CHRISTIANITY
TOPIC BOOK THREE

Reconciliation • Contrasts • Jesus • Prayer/Worship

Margaret Cooling

RMEP

RELIGIOUS AND MORAL EDUCATION PRESS

Religious and Moral Education Press
An imprint of Chansitor Publications Ltd,
a wholly owned subsidiary of
Hymns Ancient & Modern Ltd
St Mary's Works, St Mary's Plain
Norwich, Norfolk NR3 3BH

Copyright © 1992 Margaret Cooling

First published 1992
Reprinted 1993

ISBN 0 900274-27-1 spiral bound
ISBN 0 900274-28-X paperback

To Mary Bassett, who is still remembered with great affection by her ex-pupils

Designed by Topics Visual Information, Exeter

Illustrations by Jim Lester

Typeset by Exe Valley Dataset, Exeter

Printed in Great Britain by BPCC Wheatons Ltd, Exeter for Chansitor Publications Ltd, Norwich

Acknowledgements

This book is the result of six years' thinking and writing. Many different people have contributed to the development of this project, some of them without realizing they were doing so. To all of them I owe a great debt.

In the early stages Pat Travis, Arthur Rowe, Enid Mellor, Bernard Farr, Andrew Long, Suzanne Dent, Linda Smith and Sid Freeman formed a small advisory group who gave invaluable help and much-needed encouragement. For that I am exceedingly grateful to them all. Final responsibility for any errors is however mine alone.

I would also like to express my thanks to the following people for their help: Maggie Goodwin, from St Paul's School, Hereford, who worked on the National Curriculum Attainment Targets, and contributed ideas; Jean Mead for her practical and constructive suggestions, and the many teachers who offered advice and help. There are many others who contributed to this book to whom I also owe a debt of gratitude, in particular: Doris Males, Gillian Crow, Mabel Lie, Margaret Woodhall, Sue Hatherly and the staff of Stapleford House, whose patience and practical help have been a constant source of encouragement.

My thanks to the pupils of St Paul's School, Hereford and Stevenson School, Stapleford for their help in trialling this material.

Finally I wish to thank my husband Trevor, who has worked with me on this project throughout its life. Without him it would not have seen the light of day. In particular I am grateful to him for writing the introduction.

The ideas in this book were developed at Stapleford House, the Training Centre of the Association of Christian Teachers. Stapleford House also offers a school-based INSET service to primary schools providing support in the implementation of religious education. Full details of this, and other courses run at the Centre, are available from: Stapleford House, Wesley Place, Stapleford, Nottingham NG9 8DP.

ASSOCIATION OF CHRISTIAN TEACHERS

The author and publisher thank the owners or controllers of copyright for permission to use the copyright material listed below. Every effort has been made to contact copyright owners and the author and publisher apologize to any whose rights have inadvertently not been acknowledged.

The poem 'The Quarrel', by Eleanor Farjeon (page 24), is reproduced from *Silver-Sand and Sea* (published by Michael Joseph) by permission of The Estate of Eleanor Farjeon.

The song 'The Pollen of Peace', by Roger Courtney (page 29), is reproduced by permission of the Corrymeela Community.

The poem 'Palm Sunday', by Barrie Wade (**page 54**), first published in *Barley, Barley* (Oxford University Press), is included by permission of the author.

The words of the song 'Love Is Come Again', by J. M. C. Crum (page 58), are reproduced from *The Oxford Book of Carols* by permission of Oxford University Press.

The songs 'Jesu Tawa Pano', by Patrick Matsikenyiri (page 85), and 'Yesuve Saranam' (page 111) are reproduced from *Many and Great* (Wild Goose Publications).

The poems 'Prayer of the Ox' and 'Prayer of the Little Ducks' (page 107) are © Éditions du Cloître 1947, 1956. Translation © Rumer Godden 1962.

CONTENTS

INTRODUCTION

1. The Current Situation

Religious education in the primary school is at a crossroads. Under the 1988 Education Act every pupil in England and Wales is meant to receive religious education alongside the core and foundation subjects of the National Curriculum. The developing consensus is that this should take up a minimum of 5% of curriculum time.

Unlike other subjects the syllabus for religious education is determined not on a national basis, but at local level. In county and most voluntary controlled schools the local-authority agreed syllabus will be followed, whereas in voluntary aided schools the syllabus is determined by the governors. One clause in the 1988 Education Act will increasingly affect agreed syllabuses in the future. It states that, from September 1988, any *new* local-authority agreed syllabus must 'reflect the fact that the religious traditions in Great Britain are in the main Christian whilst taking account of the teachings and practices of the other principal religions represented in Great Britain'. How exactly this is interpreted and implemented will be one of the interesting features to emerge in the 1990s.

However legislation on its own is not enough to ensure that the quality of religious education is high. Evidence from a number of surveys suggests that the good practice associated with the teaching of other subjects in the primary school is frequently abandoned when it comes to religious education. We suggest there are, amongst others, three important reasons for this.

- Very few primary teachers are trained in religious education or have time to research it in the light of other pressures on them.

- The subject is potentially controversial and therefore teachers, not wishing to offend, 'play safe', resorting to formal methods of teaching.

- A lot of the published material for religious education is not written in a manner that makes it easy to use in the primary curriculum.

2. The Challenge of Primary Religious Education

Religious education is not an easy subject to teach. Of the challenges that face the teacher we shall tackle four in particular in this book:

- It is very easy for the subject to become an exercise in accumulating facts about religions with little understanding of what it means to be a believer. In particular children can rapidly come to view religion as a collection of strange stories and practices followed by rather odd people. The task of ensuring that children understand the *meaning* of these stories and practices for the religious believer can easily be ignored.

- The integration of religious themes into topic work is often superficial, with the result that they are distorted and trivialized. This usually happens because integration is planned on a word-association basis instead of at the level of the meaning of the religious material. So, for example, a project on 'fives' might include the story of David and Goliath simply because David had five pebbles in his pouch when he fought Goliath. The important theological themes of the story are ignored. Many primary teachers seem to believe that the author of Genesis was concerned with pairs, animals or water when he wrote the story of Noah! In fact he had a message about the judgement of God to share.

- It is very easy to fall between two stools when trying to relate religious material to children's experience. On the one hand teaching can be so child centred that nothing religious at all can be detected. On the other hand teachers can be so concerned to be true to the religion that they forget how alien many of the practices and stories are to young children.

- Finally, in many primary schools there is little continuity and progression in the development of religious material. Witness how familiar stories, such as 'Noah's Ark' and 'The Good Samaritan', come up again and again. In terms of the pecking order of maths, science, technology, etc., religious education is a definite loser. Religions have to be satisfied with having bits squeezed into the curriculum where there is room.

3. Meeting the Challenge

This book is the third in a series written to help the busy primary teacher overcome these problems in relation to the teaching of Christianity. It does this by developing the following characteristics in the teaching material:

- a conceptual approach;
- active learning methods;
- cross-curricular links.

A Conceptual Approach

Central to our approach is the idea that the key to understanding Christianity is a grasp of the fundamental beliefs or concepts that define Christianity and make it the distinctive faith that it is. Understanding these beliefs helps children to make sense of Christian practices.

Each book in the series covers four topics each based on a concept, or in some cases, a number of concepts, central to Christianity. The topics for Books 1–3 are:

Book 1

Sharing
Interdependence } Harvest
Giving
Peace } Christmas

Book 2

Me, My Family and Friends
The Bible
Rules
Wind, Fire, Water, Birthday of the Church

Book 3

Reconciliation } Easter
Contrasts
Jesus
Prayer/Worship

Some topics are linked to Christian festivals but all include teaching material that may be used at any time of the year.

Approaching Christianity through topics like these has major advantages, not least the opportunities for developing cross-curricular links (see below). It also provides *continuity*, both within and between topics, and helps children to develop an understanding of the underlying Christian beliefs. *Progression* is achieved by focusing on different topics, and thus different concepts, as pupils pass through the school. The process can be likened to the making of a jigsaw whereby children put the different pieces into place over the years to build up their understanding of Christianity as a whole. Furthermore a variety of activities appropriate to different levels of attainment are included for each topic.

It is particularly helpful to be able to explore the significance of the familiar Christian festivals from different angles in different years. For example, four of the ideas lying behind Christmas are:

(a) the gift of Jesus (responses to Jesus),
(b) the coming of the Prince of Peace (why Jesus came),
(c) incarnation (who Jesus was),
(d) the Light of the World (overcoming evil),

each providing a different angle for work on Christmas. The first two concepts listed correspond to the Christmas topics 'Giving' and 'Peace' in Book 1; the second two will be covered in a later volume in the series.

Active Learning Methods

It is plainly inappropriate to attempt to teach Christian concepts to primary children in a formal way using abstract theological language. It is, however, now widely accepted that children can handle religious ideas as long as they are presented in a way that makes sense in the children's world of experience. Thus Ralph Gower has pointed out in *Religious Education in the Primary Years* (Lion) that children are not going to understand a religious belief like salvation unless they have learned what it means to be saved in all kinds of other ways, from drowning by a lifeline, for example, or to feel safe and tucked up for the night. National Curriculum science adopts a similar approach. Children are introduced to the abstract concept of force at levels 1 and 2 through their own experience of

pushing and pulling. Even more so in the spiritual domain, all of us know more than we can speak about and learn through experiential methods which complement pure talk.

It is for these reasons that this book uses the creative arts, and other active learning methods, to make religious ideas accessible to children. The aim is to provide the 'feels' that make the 'tolds' fall into place or, as someone put it more technically, to provide an experience of cognitive feeling. To use these active methods successfully it is essential to remember that:

- The religious idea must not be simply tagged on to the teaching activity being used. Rather the concept should be the central focus which the active learning methods are used to communicate. In some places in this book an activity is included simply to enable the children to master a particular skill or technique. However this is never an end in itself, but only so that the children are sufficiently skilled in that technique to be able to use it as a means of successfully exploring a religious idea.

- Conversation is an essential complement to the activities if children are to advance in their understanding of religious concepts. It is most important that teachers plan to balance their use of the activities with conversation with individuals and groups, so as to encourage the children to explore the religious ideas being studied and refine their understanding of them. Conversation is a potent way of creating a concept-rich environment. Throughout the book comments are provided to give teachers ideas on how they might initiate and develop such discussion.

Cross-curricular Links

Much of the primary school curriculum, particularly outside the core subjects, is delivered through topics. This book contains four topics all with potential for cross-curricular development. Each is based on a major Christian belief and examples of work across the curriculum are given throughout. Any one of these topics will provide enough material for half a term. Alternatively each can be modified to form the basis of an RE mini-topic. Indeed we think it will be difficult to achieve an adequate RE programme without using some mini-topics.

The pressure from the National Curriculum means that an RE-focused topic may be considered an unjustifiable luxury. However it would be an impoverishment of education if pragmatic considerations were allowed to squeeze the religious dimension until its place was only that of a support to other subjects. To help teachers meet these pressures we have indicated how many of the attainment targets in the National Curriculum core subjects and in technology can be met through teaching these RE topics. The principle of integration has been to use that content and those skills from other subjects which support the development of the pupils' understanding of the Christian concept which is the focus of the topic.

A Note on Attainment Targets

Unlike other subjects there are no national attainment targets for religious education in England and Wales. However, under the terms of the 1988 Education Act, individual LEAs are allowed to adopt attainment targets in their agreed syllabus. A number of LEAs have done this. There are also several consortia which are working to give guidance to LEAs by mounting projects of national significance. The two largest are based at Westhill College in Birmingham and at Exeter University (the FARE project).

It is important to realize that this series is not an attempt to write a comprehensive RE programme and is therefore not defined in terms of attainment targets. Rather it is one contributory element to such a programme and will no doubt be used alongside other resources. At the same time teachers will be fulfilling most attainment targets in relation to Christianity by using this series. Teachers are encouraged to refer to the documents being produced by their own LEAs or the relevant national bodies in Scotland and Northern Ireland for more detail.

4. Christianity Is Not the Only Religion

This book is designed to resource the teaching of Christianity, the religion we, as authors, know best. The approach can however be applied to other religions and it is our hope that writers with expertise in different faiths will do this. The key criterion is that the ideas taught should be central to the faith being studied and that the learning activities used should always be designed to develop the pupils' understanding of these ideas. To what degree and when faiths other than Christianity should be taught is a decision that each school should take in the light of the religious make-up of its area and the educational philosophy of the staff and governors. In some church schools this series of books could form the major part of the RE programme. We expect that in most schools they will be used as part of a multifaith approach.

One point we want to emphasize is that although the ideas dealt with in this series are treated from within a Christian framework, some of them are shared with other faiths. Teachers will need to point out to pupils where this is the case. So, for example, the sanctity of the human person is central to Humanism and the belief that laws should be followed from the heart a key element in Judaism. In this series such ideas are treated as Christian beliefs and understood in a *Christian* way, because our purpose is to provide source materials for teaching about *Christianity*. It is important to understand that we are not thereby claiming a Christian monopoly of them.

Another point that is often overlooked is that Christianity is a worldwide, multicultural religion. We have tried to indicate this by including examples of Christian traditions from various cultures. Although we have focused on customs distinctive to each of these, children should also be aware that Christians across the world hold the major beliefs in common.

Finally, it has to be understood that in any approach to teaching Christian beliefs, assumptions about what Christians actually do believe inevitably have to be made. Theologians will soon tell you this is a highly controversial issue! In a book like this it is simply impossible to do justice to the wide variety of theological interpretation that exists within Christianity. What we have sought to do is isolate some of those beliefs which are shared by the majority of Christians and which are central to the traditional understanding of the faith. We are fully aware that some people will disagree with both our selection of content and the interpretation we have given it. To them we can only apologize and claim support from the fact that a primary RE book cannot attempt to be a comprehensive theological enterprise.

One particularly important difference between theologians does need mentioning. It concerns the function of Christian beliefs. Put simply, there are two main opinions. Some argue that they are attempts to describe the nature of an external ultimate reality, whilst others hold that they are ways of expressing our deepest human experiences. We have taken the former view as being that most representative of the average church member. We are however aware that there is debate about this issue amongst academics.

5. Indoctrination

Our approach is based on the premise that an understanding of Christianity is attained only when a person has insight into the meaning of the fundamental beliefs for the believer. To achieve this each one of us has to learn to cross the bridge from our own world of experience into that of the believer. In this book we help pupils do this in relation to Christianity by exploring the parallels between the child's world of experience and the particular beliefs being studied.

We wish to emphasize that this is not the same as a confessional approach, which is characterized by:

(a) the assumption that Christianity is true;
(b) the intention that children should become Christians;
(c) the involvement of children in Christian worship and experience.

However we do recognize that an educationally effective approach to teaching always carries the danger of being indoctrinatory if certain safeguards are not built in. In particular it is most important that:

- The language used by the teacher should not be inclusive. By this we mean that a phrase such as 'Christians believe that . . .' should always be used to preface a *belief* statement. If this is not done pupils may assume their assent is expected.

- Children should be encouraged to view their work as exploration of other people's beliefs unless they come from a Christian.background themselves. This will mean the teacher *protecting* the home or personal identity of the child by presenting the work as an adventure into the 'not me', thus *allowing* the child the freedom to think, 'This is not my religion.'

- In using active learning methods care should be taken not to involve children in controversial activities such as simulating sacraments, or fantasy work in contentious areas such as the events of Good Friday. Furthermore some of the activities suggested in this book will not necessarily be appropriate for all schools, and teachers should choose those most suitable for their children.

It is of fundamental importance that teachers using the approach in this book are aware of their responsibilities in this matter.

Teachers who wish to know more about the educational rationale of these materials are referred to our article 'Christian Doctrine in Religious Education', which appeared in the Summer 1987 edition of the *British Journal of Religious Education*. A further article has been submitted to *BJRE* for publication in Autumn 1992 or in 1993.

Postscript

- Some schools may not be using a topic-based approach. The majority of the ideas in this book can be used to teach religious education as a separate subject.

- All National Curriculum attainment targets specified in this book were correct at the time of going to press.

NOTES
ON USING
THE MATERIAL

1. Use of Material

A variety of activities are provided so that teachers can select those which suit their class, style of teaching and the amount of time they have available. Some material would be more suitable for church schools than for others, as noted in the text. Teachers should be careful to select the material which is most appropriate to the ethos and situation of their school.

Teacher Text/Pupil Text

The teacher text is in smaller type, like this. Sometimes the teacher text is in fairly simple language so that the teacher has to do a minimum of adaptation.

Photocopying

Any material in larger type, like this, may be photocopied for use within your school **provided** that you or the school has purchased a copy of the book. Photocopying of copies sent on inspection or borrowed from teachers' centres is **not permitted**.

It must be stressed that the photocopyable activities are not meant to function as unsupported worksheets. They have been designed so that you can 'cut and paste' to make up your own worksheets. For example, you might want to paste a story with an art activity based on it.

2. Content of Topics

National Curriculum Attainment Targets

Attainment targets for each activity are listed at the beginning of each topic. Levels are impossible to assign, however, as the material is adaptable for several age groups.

Many activities cover English attainment targets 1, 2 and 3. Often all three are indicated, but which targets are actually fulfilled will depend on how the teacher uses the material. For example, the children may read a story, have it read to them or create their own tape.

Occasionally extension work is indicated but not developed. The relevant attainment targets are specified in case the teacher wants to follow up these ideas.

Understanding the Concept

At the beginning of each topic there is a summary of the Christian beliefs central to the topic. This is background information for the teacher only. These beliefs are summarized again at various points in the topic under the heading 'Exploring Christian Belief' to indicate how they relate to the activity being used. Similar notes may appear under this heading on a number of occasions, showing which activities explore similar ideas and enabling the teacher to select whatever is appropriate to them.

Exploring Christian Belief

These sections are *not* meant to be read formally to the children. They include ideas for discussion and give the teacher information on relevant Christian beliefs. A lot of religious education occurs in the informal conversations that arise out of activities.

Notes

These sections often contain ideas which teachers might like to follow up but they are not always *directly* related to the concept being studied.

Assemblies

Assembly ideas, incorporated into the material, are designed to be 'broadly Christian' in nature. Christian comments to go with these assemblies can be found in the introduction to each topic and in the 'Exploring Christian Belief' sections. Activities are suggested for assemblies but teachers will need to add prayers, songs and the more reflective aspect of worship according to the accepted practice in their school.

The Cookery Section

The recipes included in this book have been specially adapted so that they are easy for a young child to handle. They cook relatively quickly, and good results can be achieved under classroom conditions. Traditional recipes have been simplified whilst trying to maintain the basic idea. For example the Simnel cake is a quick boiled fruit cake rather than the traditional recipe but the end result is similar. All cooking should be done with an adult, careful attention being paid to safety. Natural food colourings should be used and you can avoid fresh eggs by using dried egg if you wish.

3. Handling the Material

The Privacy of the Child

There are various activities where children can be *invited* to share their own ideas and experiences. This should never be at the expense of their privacy. Where children are asked to share, the question should be directed at a group/class so that those who want to can respond and others can stay silent without feeling out of place. If children are asked to think about personal issues it should remain a silent activity unless they specifically want to share it. They should not be asked to share publicly as someone might use the information to taunt them. A child's privacy and protection are more important than feeling we have had a good RE lesson where *everyone* shared. Some activities need sensitive handling and teachers should bear this in mind when selecting material.

The Nature of Bible Stories

This book contains many Bible stories. We have rewritten these in a form suitable for children but we have not indicated different theological interpretations. Christians divide on their interpretation of stories such as 'The Stilling of the Storm' and 'The Feeding of the Five Thousand'. Some take the story as an account of a historical incident, but also use its more symbolic meaning. Others use the symbolic meaning without pressing the historicity. Both positions are represented amongst theologians. We have left it up to teachers to decide at what age they introduce the issue of interpretation to their children. Throughout these stories, and the text, Jesus tends to be referred to as 'Jesus' rather than 'Jesus Christ' or 'Christ'. The term 'Christ' is a title, not a name, and it is more sensitive to use the name 'Jesus' where possible.

Playing by the Rules

In writing this book we have sought to follow certain rules aimed at protecting the integrity of both teacher and child. They have been mentioned elsewhere but can be summarized as follows:

- Non-inclusive language: 'Christians believe . . .' not 'We believe . . .' or 'You should believe . . .'.

- A range of activities to cover the different types of schools and occasionally alternative activities for sensitive areas.

- An avoidance of 'involvement in' certain ceremonies and other sensitive areas.

- No intrusion on the child's privacy.

4. Health and Safety

Health and safety posters should be displayed and first-aid kits should be readily available. Brief health and safety regulations are listed here but teachers are referred to their county health and safety documents for comprehensive regulations.

- All sharp knives and hot objects should be handled by an adult only.

- Candles should be well secured, lit by an adult and preferably stood in sand in a tray.

- Do not use dressed seeds and be careful handling plants – some are poisonous.

- Be careful flying kites – cables are dangerous. Wear gloves to stop friction burns and keep away from buildings and roads.

- Any moulds should be grown in sealed containers.

- Only liquid-crystal thermometers should be used, never mercury ones.

- Only new syringes should be used in science and technology and children should be taught to use tools safely.

- Take care when exploring streams and ponds. These areas can be dangerous and children must wash their hands thoroughly afterwards.

- Use only safe glues, paints and chemicals. (Consult your county document.)

- All aerosols should be used outside by an adult and should be environmentally friendly.

- Use a circuit breaker where mains electricity is used.

- Use plastic equipment not glass, and mirror card rather than mirrors.

- Children should not look directly at the sun when studying light.

- Make sure children have adequate facilities to wash their hands after certain activities.

- Observe rules of basic hygiene when handling food.

		Page	English	Maths	Science	Technology
Stories and Prayers	Saul and David	12	1			1, 3, 4
	Twins	13	2, 3			
	Joseph and His Brothers	14	1, 2			
	An Example from El Salvador	15	2, 3			
	Marie Wilson	16	3			
	Bridges	17	1		4	1, 2, 3, 4
	A Builder of Bridges: Sybil Phoenix	18	1, 2			
	Coventry	19	3			
Writing	The Agony Aunt	20	1, 2, 3			
	The Wall	21	1, 3			
	Joseph and His Brothers	22	2, 3			
Poetry	Crosses in Small Things	23	2, 3			
	An Eye for an Eye	23	2, 3			
	Quarrels	24	2, 3			
Art	Easter Trees	25	1, 2			1, 2, 3, 4
	A Class Olive Branch	26	1, 3			
	Easter Pictures	26	1			
	Birds of Peace	27	1			1, 2, 3, 4
Music	Easter Hymns	28	1, 2			
	The Pollen of Peace	29	2, 3			
	A Musical Book	30	1, 2, 3			
Drama	Wall Mimes	30	1 (3)			
	Making Friends	30	1			
	A Soap Opera	31	1, 2, 3			
PSE	Making Friends and Arguing	32	1			
Past/Present	Making Peace	33	1, 2			
Cross-curricular links	Technology and Science	34	1		3, 4	1, 2, 3, 4
	Maths	34	1	1, 2, 4		
	History	34	1, 2, 3			
	Geography	34	1, 2, 3			
Games	Easter Games	34	1			1, 2, 3, 4
Cooking	Easter Heart Biscuits	35	1, 2	2	3	

NATIONAL CURRICULUM KEY

Attainment Targets	English
1	Speaking and listening
2	Reading
3	Writing
4	Spelling
5	Handwriting
4/5	Presentation

	Maths
1	Using and applying maths
2	Number
3	Algebra
4	Shape and space
5	Handling data

	Science
1	Scientific investigation
2	Life and living processes
3	Materials and their properties
4	Physical processes

	Technology
1	Identifying needs and opportunities
2	Generating a design
3	Planning and making
4	Evaluating
5	Information Technology capability

RECONCILIATION OR MENDING FRIENDSHIPS

UNDERSTANDING THE CHRISTIAN CONCEPT OF RECONCILIATION

'Reconciliation' is the technical word for mending friendships: a difficult word but a simple concept. It can be the mending of a broken friendship with God or with others. Here are some of the Christian beliefs about reconciliation:

1. Reconciliation is primarily about the mending of the broken friendship between humanity and God. This does not mean that God is or was ever an enemy of humanity. The opposite is true. Christians believe God longed to repair the friendship and took the initiative in this, sending his Son into a hostile world to rebuild the relationship. Jesus is seen as the reconciler, the one who repaired the friendship, who brought and brings God and humanity back together.

2. It is part of being human to experience distance in relationships and separation in friendship. If a person is treated badly a barrier is built up, a barrier of hurt and resentment. The wrong that has caused the barrier has to be dealt with. It cannot just be ignored.

3. Christians believe people could not remove the wall of wrong that separated them from God. It was like painting yourself into a corner. You may have got yourself into that position but you cannot get yourself out.

4. The separation which develops when a relationship goes wrong is also described as a gorge, a gap too large to bridge. One Christian, Catherine of Sienna, described Jesus as a bridge that spanned the gap, rather like the way an intermediary can help in marriage counselling.

5. Reconciliation is about mending, joining the separated, healing the wounds caused by that separation. It is closely associated with Easter because Christians believe that, at the first Easter, Jesus conquered wrong, breaking its power. In some way he took the sins of the world upon himself and died in place of the guilty. His death wiped out the wrong of the past, removing the barrier of wrong that separated humanity and God. The description of the death of Aslan in *The Lion, the Witch and the Wardrobe*, by C. S. Lewis (Puffin), remains one of the best analogies.

6. Christians cannot explain how the death of Jesus broke the power of evil. His goodness seemed to incite hatred as well as love. Humanity did their worst and at their worst Jesus forgave them. He proved that life is stronger than death, that love is stronger than hate, and good is greater than evil. Christians cannot explain how this works though they do experience the results. They experience sin forgiven, a new friendship with God and a new power to live and overcome wrong. Christians use the word 'mystery' to describe what happened on the cross. It is rather like being able to use a word processor but not being able to explain how it works.

7. Reconciliation involves several stages: recognition of the wrong and sorrow for it; a desire to remove the barrier/bridge the gap and put right the friendship; forgiveness and acceptance of forgiveness; healing past hurts. Forgiveness is central to reconciliation, without it the friendship cannot be repaired.

8. Jesus called Christians to be reconcilers, to go out into the world and start joining the separated and making enemies into friends, spanning the gulf that separates rich and poor, black and white, men and women, etc. Examples of Christians who have responded to this call are people like Sybil Phoenix, Brother Roger and the Taizé community, McLeod and the Iona community, and groups such as Corrymeela and Prism.

9. Reconciliation is closely linked with the concept of peace. People are at peace only when their friendships are mended and whole. This topic would link to the Christmas topic 'Peace' in Book 1 in this series.

Important Note Reconciliation refers to both the mending of human friendships and the mending of the friendship with God, which focuses on Easter. This topic is so arranged that you can investigate either or both of these aspects. For example, in the Art section (pages 25–27) you will find activities with an Easter orientation and activities of a more general nature. If you select material for an Easter-based approach to reconciliation you will find the Easter story, which is needed for some activities, in the topic 'Contrasts' (pages 38–47).

Saul and David

King Saul and David were once good friends. David had killed the King's enemy Goliath and had been very successful in the army. He married Saul's daughter Michal and his best friend was Saul's son Jonathan.

Later the friendship went wrong. Saul became jealous of David. He thought David wanted to be king himself. Several times Saul's jealousy got the better of him and he tried to kill David. For safety's sake David escaped to the hills with a group of friends and lived in hiding. This was not enough for Saul. He called the army together and hunted David down.

One day David was hiding at the back of a cave when Saul entered it alone, not knowing that David and his men were there. David saw Saul and his men urged David to kill him. 'He deserves it,' they said, 'after what he has done to you.'

'Kill the King? Never!' said David. He refused to harm Saul but he crept up behind him and cut a small piece from his cloak with a knife without Saul knowing.

When Saul left the cave David came out and shouted to him. 'Saul! I was in the cave you have just left. Look! Here is a piece of your cloak. I could have killed you, in revenge for all the wrong you have done to me'.

Saul felt ashamed. 'Is that you, David?' he replied. 'You are a better person than I am. Although I have been cruel to you, you have offered me nothing but kindness. God bless you. One day you will be king.'

(*1 Samuel 24*)

Activity

Create a 'Broken and Mending Display'. As a class, collect damaged toys such as teddies whose ears have come off. Display them on a table. Make sure they are safe. There must be no sharp, broken edges.

On a second table display mending items: glue, sellotape, needle and cotton, etc.

Match up the right mending item with the right broken toy. You can make a diagram of this if you wish.

Think About It

Mending broken toys is relatively easy. How do you mend a broken friendship? Pritt-stick doesn't work on friends! What did David do to mend the broken friendship with Saul?

Exploring Christian Belief

Talk about mending friendships. How do we go about this? Forgiveness is the glue that mends a broken relationship. Discuss revenge and the pleasure there may be in this but the long-term destructiveness. Revenge is the opposite of forgiveness. David made a cold-blooded decision to repair the friendship with Saul, even though no one would have blamed him if he had killed Saul. Mending friendships is hard and difficult work; often we don't see why we should make the first move if we were in the right. It involves doing things we don't *feel* like doing. If people were to rely on feelings alone most friendships would never be mended.

STORIES AND PRAYERS

Twins

Jacob and Esau were twins but they were completely different. Esau was big and strong and loved hunting. Jacob was small and quieter and liked to stay at home. Esau was his father's favourite but Jacob was his mother's favourite.

Jacob and Esau's father, Isaac, was old, dying and nearly blind. The time had come for Isaac to pass on to Esau the special blessing that was passed from father to eldest son. Jacob decided he wanted the blessing, after all he was only a few minutes younger than his brother.

Isaac asked Esau to catch and prepare some food for a special meal. Rebecca, Jacob's mother, heard Isaac say this and she and Jacob planned to trick Esau and Isaac. Rebecca killed a goat and cooked it. Jacob tied fur on his arms so that he felt like Esau, who was very hairy.

Jacob took the food to Isaac. Isaac was surprised that it was ready so quickly. He listened to his son's voice. It did not *sound* like Esau. He felt his son's arms. The arms were hairy like Esau's, he even smelt like Esau, so Isaac passed on to his son all that he wanted. The trick had worked! All did not go well, however. When Esau came home he was so angry that Jacob had to run for his life and leave the home he loved.

Jacob fled to another country, outside Esau's grasp. There he met a girl called Rachel and was surprised to discover she was a distant cousin. Jacob met the rest of the family and his uncle, Laban, offered him work. Jacob agreed to work for seven years for nothing if he could marry Rachel at the end of that time.

The seven years went by and they seemed like only a few days because of Jacob's great love for Rachel. At last Jacob's wedding day arrived, but afterwards he found he had been tricked into marrying Rachel's sister, Leah. Brides were heavily veiled in those days.

Now Jacob knew what it was like to be tricked! He had a taste of his own medicine. Jacob complained bitterly to his uncle Laban and offered to work another seven years for Rachel. This was agreed and Jacob finally married Rachel.

Jacob was away for many years. His family grew in size and he had twelve sons and one daughter. Over the years he built up large herds of animals and became very rich.

One day God told Jacob it was time to return home. Jacob wanted to go back but he did not know what Esau would do. He wondered if Esau had ever forgiven him.

Jacob was terrified of meeting Esau and lay awake at night worrying about it. Supposing Esau still wanted to kill him? Jacob nervously went on ahead to meet his brother, but he needn't have been afraid. Esau ran to meet him, threw his arms round his brother and burst into tears of joy. Jacob had been forgiven long ago.

(*Genesis 27–33*)

Activity

Look through this story. List the good things which Jacob had when he returned home: his father's blessing etc. What was the one thing Jacob did not have which he desperately wanted?

Exploring Christian Belief

Esau could give Jacob something he wanted more than anything else, forgiveness. Esau held great power in his hands. He could either make Jacob miserable by refusing to forgive him or make Jacob happy by forgiving his brother. That is a terrible power to hold. Anyone who has been wronged and has been asked to forgive wields the same power as Esau. Explain that the blessing was very precious, it made Jacob head of the clan, a position of power. A verbal promise carried the force of law and could not be changed. Also, it was accepted practice for a man to have more than one wife.

Note Earlier Jacob had persuaded his brother to part with his 'birthright'. This was the double portion of the family wealth that would have gone to Esau as the eldest. This story is not included here but can be found in Genesis 25:27–34.

Joseph and His Brothers

Joseph was the second youngest of twelve brothers. His father, Jacob, liked him more than his brothers because he was the son of Rachel, his favourite wife. Jacob gave Joseph a special coat, far better than anything his brothers had. This made his brothers extremely jealous.

To make matters worse Joseph had some strange dreams. He dreamt that sheaves of corn bowed down to him. Then he dreamt that the stars, sun and the moon bowed down to him. Joseph believed that one day he would be an important person and many people including his own family would kneel in front of him. This really annoyed his brothers and they decided they could stand him no longer.

One day, when his older brothers had Joseph alone, they threw him down a pit and left him to die. Later some slave-traders on their way to Egypt passed by so the brothers pulled Joseph out of the pit and sold him as a slave. They dipped his new coat in goat's blood then told their father that Joseph had been killed by a wild animal.

Joseph was sold as a slave to an Egyptian called Potiphar. All went well until one day he was falsely accused of attacking his owner's wife. His master was so furious he had Joseph thrown into prison. Joseph stayed in jail, frightened and alone, for many years.

One day two men joined him in prison. Both men had strange dreams which worried them and Joseph told them what they meant. He told the baker that his dream meant he would die. He told the butler that his dream meant he would be released and go back to working for the King. The butler promised to remember Joseph when he was free but he forgot all about him until the King had two strange dreams.

Joseph was called out of prison to explain the King's puzzling dreams. Joseph told the King that his dreams meant that there would be seven years of good harvest in Egypt then seven years of bad harvest. Joseph suggested that the Egyptians collected grain in the good years and stored it ready for the bad years.

Instead of being sent back to prison Joseph was put in charge of collecting the food, and became one of the most important men in Egypt. The seven years of good harvest happened just as he had predicted. When the seven bad years came no one in Egypt went hungry. Everyone had enough to eat.

In Canaan, the land where Joseph's family lived, times were extremely hard. They had very little to eat so Jacob sent his sons to Egypt to buy grain. They never guessed that the important Egyptian who sold them corn was the little brother they had sold as a slave many years before.

Joseph wanted to be friends with his brothers again, but first he wanted to make sure they had changed. He asked a servant to plant a gold cup in one of the sacks of grain his brothers had bought. When the brothers were about to go he called out 'Stop!' and accused them of stealing. Joseph went through all the sacks and found the gold cup in Benjamin's sack. The other brothers swore that Benjamin had not taken it. He was innocent! They offered to go to prison themselves rather than lose Benjamin.

Joseph knew then that they were changed men and told them that he was their long-lost brother who they had sold as a slave. Joseph forgave his brothers and invited them all to come and live in Egypt.

(*Genesis 37–46*)

Activity

Joseph's brothers had changed, which made the healing of the friendship possible. Look closely at the story, or listen to part of 'Joseph and His Amazing Technicoloured Dreamcoat'. How did the older brothers treat Benjamin? How did they treat Joseph? How does this show that the brothers had changed?

Exploring Christian Belief

Changed behaviour helps mend a friendship. Joseph tested his brothers to make sure they had changed before he told them who he was. When Christians talk about mending the friendship with God they do not mean that God needed to change, neither do they believe that God waited for people to change for the better. He took action to mend the friendship by sending Jesus.

An Example from El Salvador

Forgiveness is part of mending friendships. This example of forgiveness in the middle of hatred comes from El Salvador.

For many years the Central American country of El Salvador was torn by conflict. Many people died at the hands of the terrible 'death squads'. One group of Salvadoreans took refuge in a crypt of a church and hid there for two years.

On All Souls Day Salvadoreans usually go to the cemetery and place flowers on the graves of loved ones who have died. The people hiding in the crypt from the death squads could not go to the cemetery, so they wrote the names of their relatives on pieces of paper and drew flowers around the names.

One poster was very strange: it was just blank lines and there were no flowers. An old man explained what it meant.

'These lines stand for the people who killed our relatives, the members of the death squads. Some of them have died too. We pray for them, but we could not bring ourselves to give them flowers.'

The war inside El Salvador has now stopped, but there is still much healing to be done before that country is one again.

Salvadoreans like the group above show that it can be done. Forgiveness can be offered to people who were 'the enemy' in order to turn them into friends.

Activity

Find out about other Christians who have forgiven their enemies in very difficult situations: for example, Corrie ten Boom from the Netherlands.

Exploring Christian Belief

Forgiveness is an integral part of mending friendships. It can help turn enemies into friends but does not always succeed in doing so. Sometimes a person can forgive the enemy but the enemy insists on remaining 'the enemy'. Please emphasize that forgiveness does not mean putting up with bullying or the bad behaviour of others. Forgiveness is not a romantic dream but a hard and practical reality. The alternatives are bitterness and strife. Evil must be opposed, even if the enemy is forgiven. When Jesus told people to forgive their enemies, he did not speak in some ideal situation. The enemy, the Romans, occupied his country, they were on the streets and armed.

Note The story of Corrie ten Boom is told in the Faith in Action series under the title *The Secret Room*, by David Wallington (RMEP).

STORIES AND PRAYERS

Marie Wilson

In 1987 an IRA bomb exploded in the small town of Enniskillen in Northern Ireland. Many townspeople had been standing watching the Remembrance Day service when the explosion happened. Amongst the crowd were Gordon Wilson and his daughter Marie, who was a nurse. Both were buried beneath the rubble and in the darkness they held hands. The rescuers rushed them both to hospital but Marie died a little later.

The loss of Marie shattered Gordon Wilson and his wife, Joan, but when interviewed Gordon publicly forgave the bombers. The Wilsons were anxious that bitterness and hatred should not rip the small town of Enniskillen apart and do more damage than the bomb.

In Enniskillen Protestants and Catholics lived side by side, and the Wilsons wanted it to stay that way. They received many messages of love and sympathy, from Catholic neighbours as well as Protestant ones.

Today Enniskillen is still at peace, there are no dividing walls down the middle of streets as there are in Belfast. Forgiveness stopped those walls from ever being built.

Activity

Using cardboard boxes build a wall. Write on the wall the things which build invisible walls between people.

Just as you can have invisible walls of fear and hatred, so you can have invisible tools that knock down those walls. The drawings below show some of the tools used to demolish real walls. Write inside them the things that demolish invisible walls.

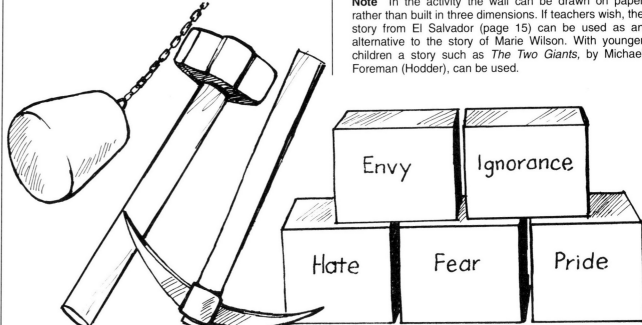

Prayer

Teach us to be demolition workers for you.
Help us to demolish walls of hatred and
    bitterness, wherever we find them.
Give us the tools we need for the job, and
    the strength to use them.

Exploring Christian Belief

When talking about the story of Marie Wilson sensitively explain the situation in Northern Ireland. Emphasize that the vast majority of Catholics and Protestants deplore the violence used in their name. Discuss the things which build walls between people and the invisible tools that knock down walls of hatred and fear: tools such as love, kindness and forgiveness.

Note In the activity the wall can be drawn on paper rather than built in three dimensions. If teachers wish, the story from El Salvador (page 15) can be used as an alternative to the story of Marie Wilson. With younger children a story such as *The Two Giants,* by Michael Foreman (Hodder), can be used.

STORIES AND PRAYERS

Bridges

An Italian Christian called Catherine once described Jesus as a 'bridge'. If you are on one side of a river and your mum or dad is on the other you need a bridge so that you can be together. Catherine said Jesus was like a bridge because he helped people get together with God, their heavenly Father. That does not mean he was literally a bridge! It is picture language. It is a way of saying that Jesus helps people meet God.

The Easter Bridge

A bridge joins two pieces of land separated by a river, a gorge, a road or some other obstacle. It spans a gap or goes over obstacles. It joins people and places that are separated.

Easter is all about Jesus joining God and people in friendship: spanning the gap and getting over the obstacle of wrong.

Activity

Take down your wall. Cross out the things which build barriers.

Using the same boxes, can you build a bridge? How many different ways can you do this?

On the sides of the boxes write the things that build bridges between people: the things that help them become friends.

Think About It

You might like to listen to the song 'Bridge over Troubled Waters', by Simon and Garfunkel, and try to think about ways in which a person can be a 'bridge'.

Exploring Christian Belief

Talk with the children about real bridges and the function they fulfil. Talk about the distance that can develop between friends. If a friend treats you badly an invisible gap appears, you feel distant and cold. Explore with the children the type of behaviour that builds bridges between people: forgiveness, love, trust etc. Sometimes someone else can bring two people together again. That person acts as a kind of bridge. Christians believe Jesus acted as a bridge to bring people back to friendship with God. Sometimes they use a picture of a cross lying across a gorge as an analogy. Particularly at Easter, Christians remember that Jesus came to mend the broken friendship with God. Often people felt God was far away and they were not good enough to be his friends. Jesus came to deal with the wrong that separated people from God. He showed them that God still loved them. The Easter story can be found in the topic 'Contrasts' (pages 38–47).

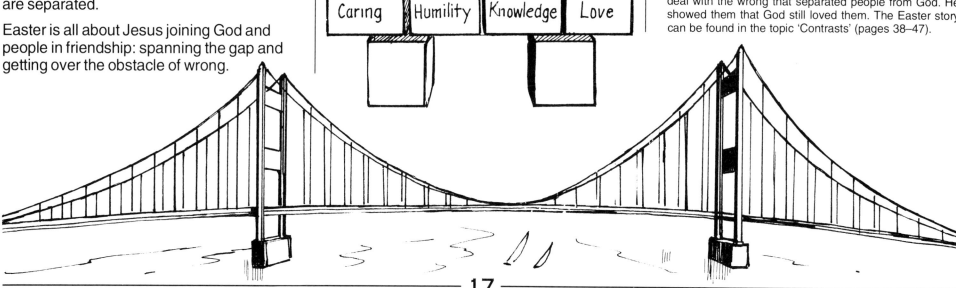

Caring   Humility   Knowledge   Love

STORIES AND PRAYERS

A Builder of Bridges: Sybil Phoenix

Sybil Phoenix was born in Guyana. At the age of ten she became a Christian.

Sybil's life was not easy. Her mother died when she was young, her father remarried and left the children with their grandfather. When she was fourteen, her grandfather died and Sybil was sent to live with an aunt and uncle who treated her like an unpaid help rather than a relative.

When Sybil was twenty she met Joe and they decided to move to Britain as many British companies were encouraging people to come to Britain at the time. When Sybil and Joe arrived they were shocked. Conditions were bad and they were often treated badly because they were black.

Eventually both Sybil and Joe found a job. They worked very long hours for very little pay. After several years Sybil gave up her job to look after their growing family and the many foster-children who were placed in their care by the Social Services.

In 1967 Sybil was asked to help out at a youth club which was having problems. Sybil agreed and started work. The youth club, later known as the Moonshot Club, was in a run-down area of Lewisham called Deptford. Often the youngsters got into trouble with the Police and Sybil spent her time trying to calm things down and keep them out of trouble. She realized many of the teenagers found it hard to get jobs because they had done badly at school, so she started various classes to help them.

In 1972 Sybil's work was recognized and she was given an MBE by the Queen. In the following years Sybil faced one tragedy after another. Her daughter Marsha was killed in a car accident. The Moonshot Club was burnt down and thirteen black teenagers were killed in a house fire in Deptford. No one knows if those fires were accidental or not, but before the Moonshot fire people were heard boasting that they would burn it down.

In the midst of these terrible tragedies Sybil still worked to bring peace. When Marsha died Sybil was comforted by both black and white friends. Any bitterness she felt about the way white people had treated her in the past melted away.

When the club burnt down Sybil was on the streets calming down the black teenagers who were angry that their club had been destroyed, and suspicious that it had not been an accident. She went from pub to pub talking to groups of youngsters, trying to keep the peace. In one pub the fighting had already started. Sybil hated pubs because the smell of beer and cigarette smoke made her feel sick. She stopped the fight in an unusual way – she was sick all over them!

Eventually the Moonshot Club was rebuilt. The new club carried on Sybil's work, but Sybil herself resigned. She went to work for an organization which helps black and white people understand each other and helps overcome prejudice. One of her colleagues described Sybil as 'a builder of bridges'.

Activity

Read through the story again. In what ways was Sybil Phoenix a builder of bridges?

Sybil's Prayer

Lord, I am tired and afraid. Yet, Lord, I know my job is simple; to love and serve you, to keep the faith, to spread your loving kindness. Lord, give me the strength to continue in your service. Amen.

Note The story of Sybil Phoenix is told in the Faith in Action series under the title *Living in Harmony*, by John Newbury (RMEP).

Coventry

In November 1940 Coventry Cathedral was bombed. There was little left of the beautiful old building of St Michael's. The next morning Jock Forbes, one of the staff, picked up two charred pieces of wood and joined them together in the shape of a cross. Later he added the words 'FATHER, FORGIVE'.

If you go to Coventry you can see the remains of the old cathedral, the charred cross and a plaque bearing a prayer with the title 'Father, Forgive'.

Father, Forgive

When hatred divides us from each other
Father, forgive.
When we long for things that belong to others
Father, forgive.
When we are jealous of other people's happiness and possessions
Father, forgive.
When our greed hurts others and ruins this world you have made
Father, forgive.
When we fail to care about the homeless and the refugee
Father, forgive.
When we use other people for our own ends
Father, forgive.
When pride causes us to trust ourselves rather than you
Father, forgive.

(*Simplified version*)

A new cathedral was opened in 1963 and became a centre for **reconciliation**. This is a long word with a simple meaning. It just means turning enemies into friends.

Before the charred cross, in the ruined cathedral, there are regular services where the words of the prayer 'Father, Forgive' are said. In the middle of a site that shows just what hatred can do, Christians declare that God forgives and that love is stronger than hate.

Activity

The reconciliation work of Coventry Cathedral still goes on. Write to the Cathedral asking them for information about their work mending friendships today. Remember to send a stamped, addressed envelope for the reply. The address is:

Coventry Cathedral Education Service
7 Priory Row
Coventry CV1 5ES

Assembly Ideas

Bring in the 'Broken and Mending Display' and match up the articles. Talk about mending friendships.

Use large boxes from the supermarket to build a wall. Write on the wall the things that build invisible walls between people. Leave the wall up.

The following day knock down the wall and tell the story of the Wilson family. Leave the boxes scattered for the next day's assembly.

Turn the boxes into a bridge and tell the story of Sybil Phoenix. Write on the sides of the boxes things that build bridges between people.

Do a sketch with one person on one side of a river and their parent on the other. Make a bridge from PE apparatus so that they can cross and be united (make this low and safe).

Play Simon and Garfunkel's 'Bridge over Troubled Waters' and talk about Jesus as a bridge.

The Agony Aunt

Dear . . . .

My friend Judith has always been my closest friend. We went to nursery school together, we were friends all through infant school and we have been friends at junior school for two years.

This term a new girl arrived in our class, Gemma. She lives near Judy and Judy always wants to include her in what we do. I got a bit fed up with trailing her around and in the end Judy and I had an argument about it and she went off with Gemma by herself. I've never been on my own before and I feel very lonely. I stand around the playground with no one to play with. I get bored at home without Judy as I have no brothers and sisters. How can I make it up with her?

Yours sincerely,

Dear . . . .

Last week I had a fight with my best friend Mark. I don't know how it happened really. It started as a silly argument and sort of grew. I hit Mark and really hurt him. He hasn't spoken to me since.

I know I was in the wrong but I don't know how to tell Mark that without feeling really stupid. I'm not even sure he would listen long enough. I worry about what happened. I could have really done some damage. Please tell me how I can put things right.

Yours sincerely,

John

Dear . . . .

Last week my friend Pat borrowed a game of mine and accidentally broke it. I was upset at the time but Pat seems almost more upset than I am. She feels very guilty and keeps avoiding me. I told her it was all right but she doesn't seem to believe me. How can I help her?

Yours sincerely,

Morag

Activity

You have probably seen the letters pages in magazines. The person who answers the letters is sometimes called an **agony aunt**.

Pretend you are an agony aunt. Choose one letter to reply to and fill in your own name in the gap. Decide what advice you would give to help mend the friendship. You might like to discuss this with a friend.

Activity

Write your own letter about an imaginary problem involving forgiveness and mending friendships. You could do this as a group and give the letter to another group to answer.

Exploring Christian Belief

Sometimes one of the hardest things about mending a friendship is forgiving yourself and accepting forgiveness. People need to be reconciled to themselves, to accept themselves as imperfect and in need of forgiveness. This does not mean that people are all bad. Christians believe people are a mixture of good and bad. Making mistakes in friendships is part of being human: 'To err is human, to forgive divine'.

WRITING

The Wall

Activity

Look at the picture. As far as the child can see there is a wall. It is so high she can't climb over it. It is so wide she can't get round it. Even if she digs down, its foundations go so deep that she can't get under it either.

The child wants to get to the other side of the wall. Describe her attempts to get round it, over it and under it. How do you think she feels?

Exploring Christian Belief

Christians believe that the wrong people do can create an invisible wall or barrier separating them from God. This barrier is too big for people to remove themselves. Christians believe God sent Jesus to smash this invisible wall of wrong because he wants people to be his friends.

Christians believe another invisible wall is erected, not a wall that divides but a wall that surrounds, a wall of love. There is a song that says this wall of love is so high you can't get over it, so wide you can't get around it, and so deep you can't get under it.

WRITING

STORY?   COVER?

Joseph and His Brothers

Activity

Read the story of Joseph. Look at the pictures. The story of Joseph is in the wrong order.

Sort the pictures into the correct order and write a caption to go under each picture to tell the story.

Exploring Christian Belief

Talk about making choices and how difficult that can be. Give the children some items to choose from. Discuss how we make ordinary choices then talk about making choices over behaviour. Joseph chose to forgive. He may not have felt like it, but he forgave. He chose to mend the friendship with his brothers rather than take revenge.

Note   The children will need a copy of the story of Joseph (page 14) for this activity.

Assembly Ideas

Turn a large sheet of paper into a wall by drawing bricks on it with large felt pens and wax crayons. Hold this up while the children's writing on 'The Wall' is read.

One child can sit behind a desk with a typewriter and read out some of the letters to an agony aunt. They can then read children's responses while pretending to type them.

Write captions for the story of Joseph (page 14) on large sheets of paper. Mix up the captions, give each one to a different child and ask the children to arrange themselves in the right order.

WRITING

Crosses in Small Things

Activity

This poem was written many years ago by a famous poet and preacher called John Donne. (His name rhymes with 'bun'.)

Who can deny me the power and liberty
To stretch my arms and my own cross
    to be?
Swim, at every stroke you are a cross,
The mast and yard make one where
    seas do toss
Look down, and spy out crosses in
    small things,
Look up, and see the birds on crossed
    wings.   *(Slightly adapted)*

Underline any words you do not understand and find out what they mean.

In this poem John Donne talks about seeing the cross shape everywhere in everyday objects. Look around you. Try to find everyday objects which make a cross shape. Draw some of these objects.

Write your own poem about seeing a cross shape in ordinary things.

Exploring Christian Belief

For Christians reconciliation is closely linked to the cross. The cross was a symbol of death and torture. Jesus gave it a new meaning. It became a symbol of love and forgiveness. It was on the cross that Jesus forgave his enemies and broke the power of evil. This is something which Christians cannot explain but they can experience. They experience forgiveness from God and the power to live as a friend of God.

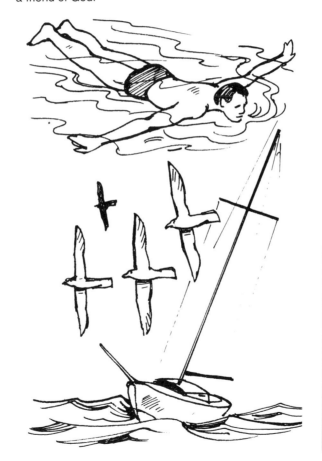

An Eye for an Eye

Activity

An eye for an eye,
A tooth for a tooth.

Can you finish this poem about revenge? Add your own ideas.

Illustrate your poem.

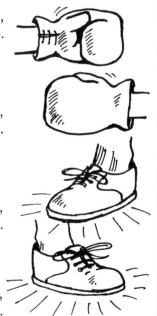

An eye for an eye,
A tooth for a tooth.
Kick for kick,
Punch for punch,
Hit for hit.

An eye for an eye,
A tooth for a tooth.
Tease for tease,
Pinch for pinch,
Stamp for stamp.

An eye for an eye,
A tooth for a tooth.
Word for word,
Stone for stone,
Hurt for hurt.
An eye for an eye,
A tooth for a tooth.

(Class poem using ideas from children at Stevenson County Primary School)

POETRY

Think About It

An eye for an eye is fair. Forgiveness is better than fairness. It gives people more than they deserve. Forgiveness says, 'Although you kicked me and it would be fair if I kicked you back, I will not.'

Activity

Jesus told people to give love in return for hatred. That is what mends friendships and turns enemies into friends.

Write your own poem about returning good for bad.

Example   A smile for a sneer,
               Love for hate.

Exploring Christian Belief

People have to forgive enemies to turn them into friends. Forgiveness goes way beyond fairness. It would have been fair for David to have killed Saul. It would have been fair for Joseph to have turned his brothers into slaves, or for Esau to have taken revenge on Jacob. Do the children think people would want total fairness? Do we really want what we deserve when we do things wrong? The rule 'An eye for an eye, a tooth for a tooth' is fair. It has been said that if we practised it the whole world would be blind and toothless. Christians believe God does not judge people as they deserve, he is more generous than that, he forgives.

Note   Please emphasize that this does not mean putting up with bullying.

Quarrels

The Quarrel

I quarrelled with my brother
I don't know what about
One thing led to another
And somehow we fell out.
The start of it was slight
The end of it was strong
He said he was right
I knew he was wrong!

We hated one another.
The afternoon turned black.
Then suddenly my brother
Thumped me on the back
And said 'Oh come along!
We can't go on all night;
I was in the wrong.'
So he was in the right!

(*Eleanor Farjeon*)

Activity

Look at the poem 'The Quarrel'. What happens between the friends? How does one person show they want to make it up?

How do you show that you want to make up a quarrel? Write your own poem about having a row and making it up.

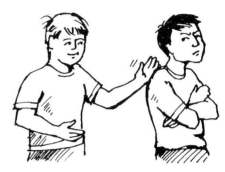

Exploring Christian Belief

Discuss with the children how difficult it is to make the first move when making up after a quarrel. Talk over the different strategies: using humour, using actions as the boy in the poem does (a playful thump), using body language. Christians believe they need to say sorry to mend their friendship with God. That initial feeling then needs working out in actions which show change. Christians believe they are not strong enough to change by themselves, so they ask God for help. They might use a prayer like this:

Almighty God who forgives all who are truly sorry
Have mercy on us.
Pardon and save us from all the things we do wrong.
Make us strong to do what is right.

(*Adapted from the Anglican liturgy*)

Assembly Ideas

Encourage the children to read the poem by John Donne and their own poems. Show the pictures which go with these. Talk about the cross symbol.

Perform a sketch which demonstrates the idea of an eye for an eye. Use the children's poems on this subject and talk about forgiveness being beyond fairness. You might like to use the story of Saul and David (page 12) as an example.

Read the poem 'The Quarrel' and encourage the children to share their ideas on making up.

Easter Trees

In countries such as Sweden, Switzerland and Holland, people have Easter trees instead of Christmas trees. Here is a simple way of making your own.

Collect twigs and small branches. Place them in a pot of wet sand.

Make some decorations from cardboard and hang them on your tree. You could use some of these symbols:

Rainbows

The rainbow is a symbol of peace and hope for the future. At Easter Christians remember that Jesus brought peace between people and God.

Doves

These are also a symbol of peace.

Crosses

There are several types of Christian cross. They can be made in white (for innocence) and/or gold (for a king). Why do you think these colours might be appropriate?

Activity

The Latin Cross

This was a sign of death but for Christians an empty cross shows Jesus has risen. It has become a symbol of love.

The Greek Cross

This is like a plus sign. The cross was a negative thing, a symbol of death. Jesus turned it into a symbol of love, something positive.

The Celtic Cross

This is a cross, the symbol of love, with a circle on top. The circle is a sign that God never ends, neither does his love.

The Maltese Cross

This has eight arms. Each of the arms stands for one part of Jesus' teaching in Matthew 5:3–10 in the Bible. Each part of that teaching starts with 'Blessed are . . .'. The word 'blessed' means 'happy'. The Maltese cross is the happiness cross.

The Russian Orthodox Cross

This has three bars. The top one is the title 'King of the Jews' given to Jesus on the cross. The longer, middle bar is the cross-beam of the cross itself. The short lowest bar is the foot-rest. The foot-rest is slanted, one end pointing to the good thief, one to the bad thief.

If you wish you can hang small eggs or sweets on the tree instead of symbols. How are you going to attach them?

Exploring Christian Belief

For Christians Easter is a time of great rejoicing, it is even more important than Christmas. That is why some Christians have Easter trees. For many Christians it is the most joyous time of the year. Children might like to design an Easter party for Christian children that will express some of this joy.

Note Use only twigs cut in pruning or already broken off. Check that all plants used are safe for children.

ART

A Class Olive Branch

Activity

Look very carefully at a branch and the way the smaller twigs are attached. Look closely at the different colours in it.

Draw your branch and colour it in using pastels. Experiment with different ways of using pastels.

- You can press lightly or firmly.
- You can use the tip or the side.
- You can mix the colours by rubbing them over each other.
- You can blend the colours.

When your branch is finished cut leaf shapes from coloured paper. Place the paper leaves on scrap paper. Colour the **edges only** by dipping just the very edges of the leaves in paint. Leave the leaves to dry.

On each leaf write something that helps make peace between friends, particularly if they have argued and separated.

Fix your leaves to your branch. Display your olive branch.

Exploring Christian Belief

An olive branch was brought back by the dove when the flood was over in the story of Noah. It became a sign of peace. In human friendships, when someone does something to show they want to make up after a row it is called 'holding out an olive branch'. Discuss the sort of 'olive branches' people hold out when they want to make up.

Note You will need to give the children a branch for this activity. Use only branches that are cut in pruning, without damaging the tree. Make sure they are safe for children.

Easter Pictures

Activity
Shadow Pictures

Cut out three crosses from thin cardboard.

Place them under some scrap paper and practise rubbing gently over the top with crayons, used sideways, until you can get a good shadow-rubbing.

From the same card, cut out clouds and a hill (big enough to take three crosses). Using black crayons practise making shadow-rubbings as before.

Place the hill, clouds and crosses underneath a piece of kitchen paper to form a Good Friday scene. When you have them in an arrangement you like, rub carefully with a black crayon to make a shadowy picture. You may need a friend to help you.

When your rubbing is finished use very watery paint to go over your picture. What colour do you think would be suitable?

ART

Think About It

Look at your picture. It is very shadowy. Good Friday is a very sad day for Christians yet they call it **Good** Friday.

Good Friday is a suitable name for this sad day because Christians believe that on Good Friday Jesus was doing something good. He was dealing with the wrong that spoilt people's friendship with God.

Good Friday may have originally been called God's Friday.

Activity

Adding Hope

The rainbow is a symbol of peace and hope. How could you add a rainbow to your picture?

Exploring Christian Belief

Although Good Friday is a sad day for Christians, it is also a day of hope, a day when they remember that the cross was not the end of the story. For Christians the cross is a sign of victory, because it represents the defeat of evil.

Birds of Peace

Activity

The dove is a symbol of peace. A bird with the body of a dove and human hands for wings could be a symbol of peacemaking. Here is one way to make a dove like this.

Draw round your hands on white paper and cut the drawings out.

Draw a simple body of a white dove and cut it out. Make sure it is the right size for the hand shapes to be its wings.

Arrange the body and the hand 'wings' of the dove on dark paper. Glue them down.

You could also do this by using white handprints. Can you think of other ways of making a dove with hand shapes as wings?

Exploring Christian Belief

The dove is a Christian symbol of peace but this dove has human hands for wings. Jesus called people to be peacemakers, to turn enemies into friends. Talk with the children about how people can be peacemakers. How can *they* be peacemakers? Christians think of Jesus as the great peacemaker. At Easter Christians remember that he mended the friendship with God, bringing peace between God and humanity.

Note Use paint safe for handprints.

Assembly Ideas

Make a large olive branch in assembly and add a leaf each day, exploring through stories the different things that help to make peace between people.

Make a bird of peace in assembly and run a series on peacemakers.

Make an Easter tree. Each day a different child could make a symbol and place it on the tree, explaining its meaning.

Make a large shadow-rubbing of a cross in assembly and add a rainbow. Talk about why Good Friday is 'Good'.

ART

Easter Hymns

Easter is a time when Christians remember that Jesus mended the friendship between God and human beings. Below are two popular Easter hymns, each with a story to it.

When I Survey the Wondrous Cross

When I survey the wondrous cross
On which the Prince of glory died,
My richest gain I count but loss,
And pour contempt on all my pride.

Forbid it, Lord, that I should boast
Save in the cross of Christ my God;
All the vain things that charm me most,
I sacrifice them to His blood.

See, from His head, His hands, His feet,
Sorrow and love flow mingled down;
Did e'er such love and sorrow meet,
Or thorns compose so rich a crown?

Were the whole realm of nature mine,
That were an offering far too small;
Love so amazing, so divine,
Demands my soul, my life, my all.
(*Isaac Watts*)

This hymn was written by Isaac Watts, who lived from 1674 to 1748. One day, when he was about twenty, Isaac complained to his father that the singing at church was boring. His father told him to write his own hymns if he thought he could do better.

Isaac was always keen to try something new. He had learned Latin at the age of four, Greek at nine, French at ten and Hebrew at thirteen. Now he started writing hymns, and he wrote nearly 750 of them. 'When I Survey the Wondrous Cross' is generally thought to be his best, and is frequently sung at Easter.

There is a Green Hill Far Away

There is a green hill far away,
Without a city wall,
Where the dear Lord was crucified,
Who died to save us all.

We may not know, we cannot tell,
What pains He had to bear;
But we believe it was for us
He hung and suffered there.

He died that we might be forgiven,
He died to make us good,
That we might go at last to heaven,
Saved by His precious blood.

There was no other good enough
To pay the price of sin;
He only could unlock the gate
Of heaven, and let us in.

O dearly, dearly has He loved,
And we must love Him too,
And trust in His redeeming blood,
And try His works to do.
(*Mrs C. F. Alexander*)

Mrs Alexander (1818–1895) lived and worked in Ireland. She wrote this hymn while sitting at the bedside of a child who was very ill. The little girl eventually recovered and always regarded this hymn as hers in a special way.

The hymn was published in a book called *Hymns for Little Children*. The tune for the hymn was written by a friend of the composer Mendelssohn and was very popular. The money from the sales of this book went to a school for children who were deaf or had speech difficulties.

Activity

Look at the words of these two hymns. Find one line in each hymn that expresses the love and forgiveness of God.

Activity

Find some more popular Easter hymns. Look especially for Easter hymns which have been written this century.

MUSIC

The Pollen of Peace

Words and music by Roger Courtney
© 1980 The Corrymeela Community

This song comes from the Corrymeela Community, which works for peace and reconciliation in Ireland, though the words can apply to other situations.

Children might like to write to Corrymeela for more information. Remember to send a stamped, addressed envelope for the reply. The address is:

The Corrymeela Community, Corrymeela House, 8 Upper Crescent, Belfast BT7 1NT, Northern Ireland.

A Musical Book

Stories of reconciliation such as *The Two Giants*, by Michael Foreman (Hodder), can be turned into musical books. *The Two Giants* is about the right length for this.

Read the story to the children until they know it well. Next go through each page with the children asking them what instruments could be used for different parts of the story. For example:

- Nightingales singing – recorders
- Waves crashing on the shore – drums and cymbals

Organize groups or individuals to play the instruments. Each group can have cards with word or picture cues (depending on the age of the children) to remind them when to play their instruments.

Practise reading the book with the children adding their music. For example:

- 'Sam leapt onto the first rock. Then he leapt out onto the second rock' – woodblocks for footsteps
- 'Boris opened one giant eye' – scrapers

Discuss with the children whether they need a conductor or not. If they do want a conductor, they will need to agree on signals which they will all understand and follow. Pupils can research how orchestras are conducted.

MUSIC

When you have practised the complete musical story, children might like to add drama to it. Alternatively, different scenes can be drawn on acetates and shown on an overhead projector as the story progresses.

Note With older children a pupil can take the part of the teacher and read the story.

Assembly Ideas

Perform your musical story.

Sing the Corrymeela song and other songs about reconciliation or invite some Christians in to sing them. If the children have sent for information about Corrymeela, ask them to share what they have found out about this group.

Play recordings of the two Easter hymns in assembly and tell the stories behind them, or sing them if appropriate.

Wall Mimes

Mime can be an extremely effective art form but actions have to be studied very carefully.

Building a Wall

Discuss what is needed for building a wall. What processes would builders go through? What actions are needed?

Ask the children to work in groups as building gangs to mime building a wall.

When they have finished the children can become demolition gangs and mime knocking the wall down. Once again take them through the movements carefully.

The Invisible Wall

This is a mime where the children walk along only to hit an invisible barrier. They must feel their way along the barrier to see if they can get over it or under it or around it.

The children can then do this in pairs, one each side of the wall, both feeling their way but unable to meet.

Exploring Christian Belief

Talk with the children about the invisible walls people build: walls of fear, hatred and prejudice, walls of selfishness and pride. How can those walls be taken down? What demolishes them? Christians believe that an invisible barrier or wall existed between God and humanity, a barrier consisting of the wrong people had done. Christians believe Jesus removed this barrier and made it possible for people to be close friends with God.

Note A writing activity to go with this can be found on page 21.

Making Friends

Ask the children, in pairs, to express friendship in movement. For example:

- Weaving movements, weaving the two people together
- Revolving movements where the children revolve around each other
- Movements made face to face
- Joining movements, dancing with one part of the body joined (hands, arms, etc.)

In pairs, the pupils can then express the friendship breaking up. For example:

- Weaving movements with the pair gradually separating
- Revolving movements with the children spinning apart
- Movements made back to back
- Starting the dance joined then breaking away

The friendship can then be rebuilt.

MUSIC

DRAMA

A Soap Opera

Activity

As a class, turn the story of Jacob and Esau or Joseph and his brothers into a serial or **soap opera**. You can find out more about these two stories by reading a children's Bible.

Break up the story into different episodes in a way that will make the audience want to watch the next episode. The two lists suggest how this might be done but these are only examples. You may want to divide up your story differently.

Share out the different episodes among small groups. Each group then writes up their episode as part of a script for a soap opera. Bring out the jealousy, resentment and the forgiveness at the end.

When the complete script is finished choose people to act the parts and produce your 'soap'.

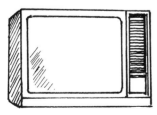

Jacob and Esau

One way to divide this story into episodes would be:

1. Favouritism. Mum favours Jacob, the quiet, brainy and somewhat crafty one; Dad favours Esau, more brawn than brains.
2. Planning the trick
3. Fooling Dad
4. The great escape
5. Marrying the wrong bride
6. Going home

Joseph and His Brothers

One way to divide this story into episodes would be:

1. The spoilt brat
2. The dreamer
3. Sold as a slave
4. Thrown into jail
5. The butler and the baker
6. Pharoah's dreams
7. Joseph as minister for food
8. The chance for revenge

Exploring Christian Belief

Discuss favouritism with the children. Talk about the problems favouritism causes in the story used. In both stories there is the chance for revenge. Both Joseph and Esau are badly wronged and Joseph's brothers and Jacob are only too aware that their brother has the right to revenge. Forgiveness heals the broken relationship. Discuss the decision to forgive with the children. If Joseph or Esau had decided on revenge it would have been a very different story – and a much longer soap opera!

Note   The children will need a copy of the story of Jacob and Esau (page 13) or Joseph (page 14) and/or a children's Bible for this activity. Other stories about forgiveness could also be made into soap operas, provided that children have access to a version containing sufficient potential episodes.

Assembly Ideas

Perform a different episode of the soap opera each day. If possible create a theme tune to introduce the soap opera.

Perform the invisible-wall mime, then build walls of boxes, writing on them the different things which build barriers between people.

DRAMA

Making Friends and Arguing

Discussion

Put the children into groups of 4–6 and ask them to discuss arguments:

- What sorts of things cause arguments?
- How do people feel when they argue?
- Should arguments always be avoided?
- How do you go about making up?
- Would a peacemaker help?

Introducing Peacemakers

Select several children to be peacemakers. Repeat the arguing activity but this time send in a peacemaker when the children start to argue.

Discussion

What difficulties did the peacemakers face? Was it easy for the children arguing to accept a peacemaker? What would have to happen for a peacemaker system to work?

Exploring Christian Belief

Jesus told Christians to go out into the world and be peacemakers. Peacemakers often get misunderstood and their job is extremely difficult. Jesus was a peacemaker and some people hated him. Terry Waite was a peacemaker and was taken hostage. Allan Boesak, who works to bring peace in South Africa, maintains that Christians in his country have to be prepared to face great suffering to bring peace. If the children are going to act as peacemakers they must understand that they will not always be popular. Some people prefer to stay enemies!

Warm-up

Initially the children should walk round the room changing direction when you clap. After a while ask them to get into pairs when you clap but to continue walking.

Next say that each time you clap again they must find a new partner to walk with. Do this many times until the children have got the hang of changing partners, rather like an 'excuse me' waltz.

You will need an even number of children for this or to be prepared to join in yourself.

Arguing

Put the children in pairs. Ask them to pretend to be playing together.

Now ask them to argue. Something must happen in the game to cause an argument.

The friends separate and find another person to play with.

After playing for a while the new pair argue, split up and find other friends. Do this as many times as you wish.

PSE

Making Peace

Our countries share a border and many years ago they nearly went to war. This is the story of what happened.

Christ of the Andes

The border between Chile and Argentina passes through the Andes, a high range of mountains which run the length of South America. These mountains are rich in silver and copper so it matters where the border is.

At the beginning of this century no one was quite sure where the border ran, and the two countries argued over where it should be drawn. As the argument grew, so the two countries armed. The more money their governments spent on weapons, the poorer the people became. Slowly each country prepared for war.

Fortunately, the leaders of Argentina and Chile realized in time that it would be stupid to go to war over this issue. Instead they asked two people who did not belong to either Chile or Argentina to draw the boundary for them.

When the border was eventually decided the people promised to abide by the decision. They also melted down their metal cannon and built a huge statue of Jesus, which was placed at a high point in the mountains. Underneath the statue is written:

Sooner shall these mountains crumble than the people of Argentina and Chile break the peace, which at the feet of Christ the Redeemer, they have sworn to keep.

Activity

Look up South America on a map. Find out where Chile, Argentina and the Andes mountains are.

Why do you think the people chose to build a statue of Jesus from the weapons they had melted down?

Think of present-day troublespots. If people were to melt down their weapons today, where would be a suitable place to put a similar statue?

Cross-curricular Links

Technology and Science

Building Bridges

Ask the children to design a bridge that will span a 30 cm gap and will be strong enough to take a 50 g weight in the centre. They can use materials available in the classroom such as paper, card, wood and construction sets (Meccano etc). Can they make a soft material such as rope, paper or card strong enough to be used in a bridge? You could suggest they experiment with folding to increase strength.

Alternatively, the children can make a simple plank bridge and then experiment with variables:

- Changing the materials
- Changing the means of support
- Changing the thickness of the plank
- Changing the position of the supports
- Putting the plank on its side

Children can also investigate how the load changes when a vehicle crosses the bridge.

Building Walls

Ask the children to build a wall 15 cm high from construction bricks (Lego etc.) using the strongest pattern they can. How could they test their wall?

What is the most common pattern of bricks? Is this the best pattern? What gives it its strength? What shape is a brick? Why do the children think it is this shape? Why do they think some bricks have holes?

If possible go out and look at the bridges/walls in the area. Invite a civil engineer to talk to the class about bridge-building.

Maths

Distance, weight, shapes and angles will all be involved in the design of bridges.

History

Children could investigate early bridges such as clapper bridges and the development of bridges, famous bridge-builders such as Brunel and Telford, or bridge disasters such as the collapse of the Tay Bridge.

Look at people in the past who worked to bring communities together. The Euro Tunnel could also be discussed.

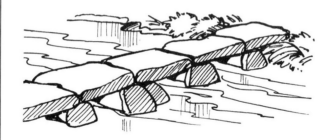

Geography

What sort of terrain has to be spanned by bridges (e.g. gorges, rivers, marshes, valleys, the sea)? What happens when communities are isolated from each other?

Useful Books

The Two Giants, by Michael Foreman (Hodder).
The Selfish Giant, by Oscar Wilde (Ladybird).
The Way to Sattin Shore, by P. Pearce (Puffin).
King Nimrod's Tower, by Leon Garfield (Methuen).
Stories from the Christian World, by David Self and Nick Harris (Macdonald).
The Bronze Bow, by E. Speare (Gollancz).
The Easter Book, by A. Fancombe (NCEC).
The Lion Easter Book, by M. Batchelor (Lion).

Easter Games

At Easter Christians celebrate Jesus mending the friendship between people and God. Easter is a joyous festival. It is celebrated with special food, special services and games. Football, skipping and marbles are all played at Easter.

Hide and Seek Eggs

In Italy long strings are attached to painted eggs and the eggs are hidden, with only the strings showing. Children have to follow the strings to find the eggs.

Activity

Make your own papier mâché eggs for the Italian Hide and Seek Game.

Paste torn-up newspaper around the outside of small balloons, building it up slowly in layers. Use a water-based glue and allow each layer to dry before you add the next.

When the paper is dry, pop the balloons and paint the eggs. Decorate them with colourful patterns.

How are you going to attach the string? You could use coloured wool instead of string.

Activity

Design a game suitable for a Christian family to play as part of their Easter celebration. It can be an indoor or an outdoor game. It can be quiet or noisy. It does not matter as long as the game is fun, safe and joyful.

When you have written your game ask some friends to test it out. Make any improvements you need to.

Exploring Christian Belief

For Christians, Easter is the most joyful time of the year. They celebrate being friends with God and being forgiven. In some ways it is a sad time for they remember that Jesus died so that people could be friends with God, but Christians believe Jesus rose from the dead and is still alive to be people's friend.

Note The children's games could be offered to a local church as ways to celebrate Easter at home. Make sure the glue used for the papier mâché is safe.

Easter Heart Biscuits

Activity

You will need

100 g butter or solid margarine
100 g caster sugar
2 egg yolks
225 g plain flour
boiled sweets

mixing-bowl
wooden spoon
foil
rolling-pin
heart-shaped cutters (two sizes) or a
   circle and a heart shape
baking-tray
wire rack

Method

1. Cream the butter and sugar together.

2. Add the egg yolks and beat them in.

3. Add the flour and mix to a firm dough, adding a little water if too dry.

4. Wrap the mixture in foil and place in the fridge for 30 minutes.

5. Ask an adult to set the oven to gas mark 5/190°C (375°F).

6. Roll out the mixture on a floured board until it is 3 mm thick.

7. Cut out hearts using the larger cutter then cut a smaller heart from the centre of each.

8. Line a baking-tray with foil and place the biscuits on the tray.

9. Place a boiled sweet in the centre of each biscuit.

10. Bake for 7–8 minutes or until golden.

11. Leave to cool on the tray. When almost cool peel off the foil and place the biscuits on a rack to finish cooling.

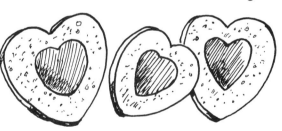

Think About It

Why do you think heart-shaped biscuits would be appropriate for a Christian family celebration at Easter?

GAMES

COOKING

		Page	English	Maths	Science	Technology
Stories and Prayers	Palm Sunday	38	1, 2			
	Monday	40	1, 2, 3			1, 3, 4
	Tuesday	41	1, 2			
	Wednesday	41	1, 2			
	Thursday	42	1, 2, 3			1, 2, 3, 4
	Good Friday	44	3			
	Saturday	46	1, 3			
	Easter Sunday	47	1, 2			
Writing	Newspaper Stories	49	1, 2, 3			5
	The Coin, Leaf and Feather	50	3			
	Untold Stories	50	2, 3			
Poetry	Easter Haikus	51	2, 3			
	An Easter Cinquain	52	3			
	Colour Poems	52	1, 3			
	The Song of . . .	53	2, 3			
	Easter Poems	54	1, 2, 3			
Art	Water-bugs and Dragonflies	55	1, 2			
	Split Pictures	56	1, 2			
	Wax Pictures	56	1, 2			
	Topsyturvy People	57	1, 2			
Music	Easter Carols	58	1, 2			
	Music for Easter	59	1, 2			
Drama	Greetings	60	1, 2			
	Contrasts in Movement	61	1			
	Ways of Understanding	61	1			
PSE	Badges	62	1			1, 2, 3, 4
Past/Present	Easter Around the World	63	1, 2			
Cross-curricular links	Easter Flowers	64	1, 2		2	
	Geography	64	1, 2			
	Science	64			1, 2, 3, 4	
	Maths	64		1, 2, 3, 4, 5		
	Technology	64				1, 2, 3, 4
Games	Orange Rolling	65		1, 2	1, 4	
	Egg Cracking	65	1			
Cooking	Quick Hot Cross Buns	66	1, 2	2	3	
	Easter Bread	67	1, 2	2	3	

NATIONAL CURRICULUM KEY

Attainment Targets	English
1	Speaking and listening
2	Reading
3	Writing
4	Spelling
5	Handwriting
4/5	Presentation

	Maths
1	Using and applying maths
2	Number
3	Algebra
4	Shape and space
5	Handling data

	Science
1	Scientific investigation
2	Life and living processes
3	Materials and their properties
4	Physical processes

	Technology
1	Identifying needs and opportunities
2	Generating a design
3	Planning and making
4	Evaluating
5	Information Technology capability

CONTRASTS

UNDERSTANDING CHRISTIAN CONCEPTS ABOUT EASTER

This topic uses an umbrella title not a Christian concept. It is a way of looking at Easter and at human behaviour. The following Christian beliefs are explored in this topic:

1. Christians (along with many others) believe that good and evil are opposites. Although they may be opposites they are not equal in strength. Good is stronger than evil. Love is stronger than hate. Life is stronger than death. The Easter story shows up these stark contrasts.

2. Jesus was a person who demanded a response. People were not neutral about him. In the Easter story those responses come to the surface.

   - He is welcomed and loved on Palm Sunday at his entry into Jerusalem. He is rejected and hated as the crowds call for his crucifixion on Good Friday.
   - His friends, who have stuck loyally by him and say they are ready to die for him, run away when he is arrested. Peter denies ever knowing him. Judas moves from friendship to betrayal.
   - The hatred of the crowds stands in contrast to the forgiveness of Jesus: 'Father, forgive, they don't know what they are doing.'
   - The grief and despair of Good Friday give way to the joy and hope of Easter morning. Life triumphs over death.

   - The righteous anger shown when Jesus throws the money-changers out of the Temple stands in contrast to his calm acceptance of his arrest.

3. There are well-known analogies that are used to help children understand these contrasts in the Easter story:

   - The 'tomb' of the egg and the birth of the chick
   - The 'death' of the caterpillar in the chrysalis and the vibrant beautiful butterfly
   - The change from water-bug to dragonfly
   - The darkness of night (death) and the light of day (life)
   - The 'death' of winter and the life of spring
   - The 'death' of the seed and the life of the plant

   Use those analogies which you find useful and appropriate. They do, however, need tying into the story of Jesus as many of these symbols have lost their Christian meaning in our secular society.

4. The contrasts in the Easter story are reflected in the worship of the Church. Churches differ in their practices. In some all decoration is removed on Good Friday. In others all brass is covered and only dark or drab colours of mourning are allowed during Lent. The bells are silent during Holy Week or ring a death toll. On Easter Sunday churches are decorated with yellows and whites. Flowers are there in profusion and the bells ring out a message of hope and joy.

5. This particular topic uses 'Contrasts' to look at Easter. This theme could be investigated at any time of year using different stories but similar activities. For example, colour poems (page 52) can be used to explore joyful/sad emotions in other contexts. Here are some alternatives from the Bible:

   - Obedience and disobedience: the two sons (Matthew 21:28–32)
   - Love and hate: David and Jonathan contrasted with Saul (1 Samuel 20–21)
   - Justice and injustice: Naboth's vineyard (1 Kings 21) and the cleansing of the Temple (Mark 11:15–19)
   - Forgiveness and lack of forgiveness: the two debtors (Matthew 18:21–35)
   - People whose lives changed: Jacob, Joseph, Zacchaeus, Paul
   - Compassion and apathy: the Good Samaritan (Luke 10:25–37)

Palm Sunday

On the first Palm Sunday people tore down branches and laid them at Jesus' feet, hailing him as king. In less than a week they were calling for his death.

Christians often read the story of the last week of Jesus' life in the week before Easter. This week of stories contains many different reactions to Jesus.

The Entry into Jerusalem

Jesus knew his life would soon come to an end, but he deliberately went to Jerusalem, where his enemies were waiting for him.

He entered the city riding on a donkey, an animal of peace, rather than a war-horse.

Crowds lined the streets and started shouting 'Hosanna' and 'God bless the king.' They tore branches from the trees and threw them down for the donkey to walk on. Some pulled off their coats and spread them out to make a carpet.

The religious leaders were shocked. 'Tell the crowd to shut up,' they snapped.

Jesus looked at them sadly, 'If I told the crowd to be quiet,' he said, 'even the stones would start shouting.'

When the excitement of the day was over Jesus went back to Bethany, a small village outside Jerusalem, to the home of Lazarus, Martha and Mary, some of his closest friends. (*Luke 19:28–40*)

Activity

How do you welcome people? Find out different ways of welcoming people.

Exploring Christian Belief

Talk about making people feel welcome. How do the children make new members of the class feel welcome? What sort of people would they cheer? Discuss with the children why the religious leaders wanted the crowds to be quiet. Why was Jesus so popular with the ordinary people? Jesus chose a donkey, a symbol of peace, rather than a horse, a symbol of war. Christians call him the Prince of Peace. Bring out the contrasts between the reactions of the people and the religious leaders.

STORIES AND PRAYERS

Activity

Christians remember Palm Sunday in many different ways. In northern Europe sallow willow is often used to decorate homes and churches instead of palm, as palm does not grow in cold climates.

Palm crosses are given out in many churches and are kept until the beginning of Lent the following year. Follow the instructions for making your own 'palm' cross.

1. Cut two strips from a large sheet of sugar paper, each 2 cm wide.

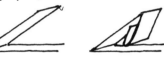

2. Take one piece of paper. Fold up the first 2½ cm then fold it over twice more.

3. Take the other end of this piece of paper and form a circle with it. The end should be **behind** the folds and the folds should be on the outside of the circle.

4. Pinch the circle together at the join and flatten the loops. This makes the cross-beam of the palm cross.

5. Take the other piece of paper. Snip one end into a point.

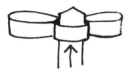

6. Push the pointed end through the middle of the folds in the cross-beam until you can just see it poking through. Fix this with a little Pritt-stick if you need to.

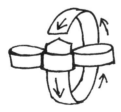

7. Bend the other end up, behind the cross-beam and back down through the folds.

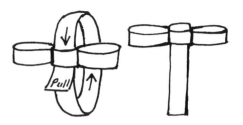

8. Pull it gently until it tightens then flatten it.

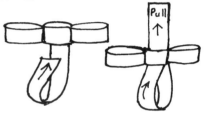

9. Bend the end of the paper up again and push it through the front of the folds but do not pull it tight. Leave enough paper to make a loop about the same size as the arms of the cross-beam. Flatten the loop.

10. This should leave you with a longer piece for the base of the cross. You can trim this into a point.

STORIES AND PRAYERS

Monday

Clearing Out the Temple

The next day Jesus went to the Temple to pray. As he entered the Temple he noticed the many stalls which sold animals. What really attracted Jesus' attention, however, were the stalls of the money-changers, for only special Temple money could be put into the Temple collecting-boxes.

Jesus noticed that many of the stall-holders were cheating the poor out of what little money they had. Jesus was angry that the poor should be treated in this way, especially in the house of God, a God of truth and love. He was also angry that the courts of the Temple, a place which was used for prayer, had been turned into a market.

Jesus walked up to the money-changers and turned over their tables, scattering their money everywhere. He drove out the animals and the stall-holders with them.

'My Father's house should be a house of prayer,' he said. 'You have made it into a den of robbers.'

The money-changers and the Temple authorities were furious. They hated Jesus. 'Who gave him the right to do this?' they said to each other. 'Just who does he think he is?'

Jesus made many powerful enemies that day who began to plot his death.

(*Luke 19:45–48*)

Think About It

Do you think it is right to have a market in a special 'sacred' place? Would it be right to have a shop in a church? Do you think it is all right to sell Bibles in a church? Would it be right to sell ice cream?

Activity

Make an Easter diary with eight pages. Each page must be a different colour and slightly larger than A4. How are you going to make your book?

Write a day of the week at the top of each page, starting with Palm Sunday. Mount your work on the correct pages.

Activity

What makes you angry? Have you ever felt anger when you have seen other people being treated badly?

Find out about people whose anger has made them change the world for the better: people such as General Booth, the founder of the Salvation Army.

Exploring Christian Belief

Jesus got very angry when he saw people being cheated and he channelled that anger into action. The Bible never says that anger is wrong when it is used for others and does not lead to uncontrolled violence. Controlled anger on behalf of others has led many to put right various wrongs in the world. Biographies can be used to look at some of God's angry people whose anger led them to fight against wrong. The Faith in Action series (RMEP) is a good source for these. Bring out the contrast between Jesus as the Prince of Peace when he entered Jerusalem and the stormy scene in the Temple. Peace is not papering over the cracks. Sometimes you have to disturb a superficial peace to bring about a deeper peace.

Tuesday

Questions

The next day various people questioned Jesus. They were hoping to trick him into saying something that would get him into trouble, but Jesus replied to all their questions very carefully.

Finally a teacher asked Jesus what the two most important laws were. Jesus replied, 'Love God and love your neighbour.'
(*Matthew 22:34–40; Luke 10:25–28*)

Activity

Jesus told a story about neighbours. Read Luke 10:25–37 in the Bible to find out who Jesus said were neighbours.

Neighbours

When you said 'Love your neighbour'
Did you really mean all of them?
'Love your neighbour' sounds very nice,
But my neighbours are a bit difficult to love.
The lady next door is always shouting at us,
And she never lets us have our ball back if it
   goes in her garden.
I don't mind loving my neighbour
As long as it means the old lady who always
   sends us sweets at Christmas.
When you said 'Love your neighbour'
Did you *really* mean all of them?

Exploring Christian Belief

The word 'neighbour' applies to all, as Jesus made clear in the parable of the Good Samaritan. Talk about the meaning of the word 'love'. Here it is very much a way of life and a way of behaving, not just a sentimental feeling. Discuss why some people are difficult to love. Bring out the contrasting responses in the story of the Good Samaritan (see *Christianity Topic Book 1*, pages 18 and 20).

Wednesday

Two Women Who Gave

Jesus sat in the Temple watching people put money in the chests that were used for collections. Many rich people went by and put in large amounts, then a poor widow came along and put in two very small coins.

Jesus noticed the woman and said to his friends, 'That widow has put in more than all the rich people. They gave but still had lots left over. She gave everything she had.'
(*Luke 21:1–4*)

In the evening Jesus was eating at a friend's house when a woman came in. She was crying and very upset. The woman took out a very expensive alabaster jar of perfume and poured it over Jesus' head.

Some people got very angry. 'What a waste! That perfume could have been sold and the money given to the poor,' they said.

'Stop bothering this woman,' said Jesus. 'She knows I am going to die and she has done this to show her love and sorrow. The poor will always be with you, but I will not.'
(*Matthew 26:6–13*)

41

Thursday

The Last Supper

Activity

Look closely at both stories. What 'invisible gift' did the widow give as well as the two coins? What did the woman with the alabaster jar give besides the very expensive perfume?

The Widow's Gift: A Meditation

He did not hear the lightness of the noise
As the two delicate coins dropped.
Their weight so small they hardly chinked.
To him they were heavy with the weight of
    love
As they crashed against their larger
    brothers of silver and gold.

Thank you, Father, that when we give you do not listen for the chink of coins, or look on the size of the gift, but only at our hearts.

Exploring Christian Belief

Discuss with the children the two different gifts and the invisible gifts such as love and worship. More ideas on invisible gifts can be found in the topic 'Giving' in *Christianity Topic Book 1*. Contrast the monetary value of the two gifts in these stories. The jar of perfume was worth nearly a year's wages. It could have been sold and the money given to the poor. Were the disciples right to criticize the woman? Why on this occasion did Jesus accept the rich gift when he normally put the poor first?

Before he died Jesus wanted to be alone with his friends and share a special farewell meal with them. He took the bread and wine, thanked God for it then shared it among his friends. He told them that in future they were to do this to remember him. The bread and wine were a reminder of his death and a sign of a new friendship with God.

The disciples did not really understand what he was talking about. What had bread and wine to do with their friend Jesus? Jesus knew they were puzzled, he also knew he was going to die, and he was giving them a special way of remembering him.

Jesus was very sad during this meal. Not only did he know it was the last time he would eat with his friends, he also knew that one of his friends would betray him. He looked at his disciples and said to them, 'One of you will betray me tonight.'

The disciples were shocked and stared at each other in disbelief, each one denying that they would ever do such a thing.

'I'll never leave you,' boasted Peter. 'I am willing to die for you.'

'Peter, you don't know what you are saying,' replied Jesus. 'Before the cock crows you will deny you ever knew me.'

Jesus knew Judas would betray him, so he turned to him and whispered, 'What you are about to do, do quickly.' Judas quietly left the room.

After the meal Jesus took a towel and washed his disciples' feet. Peter objected because it was the job of the lowest servant.

'If I don't wash you, Peter, you cannot be my disciple,' said Jesus.

'Then wash all of me,' exclaimed Peter.

Jesus smiled and replied, 'No, just your feet will be enough!'

When Jesus had finished he looked at their confused faces and said, 'I know you don't understand what I have done, but one day it will all make sense. You call me your Lord and Teacher. That is right, but if I, your Lord, can wash your feet, in the same way you can wash each other's feet.'

(*Luke 22:14–20; John 13:1–30*)

Activity

Jesus gave the disciples a way of remembering him: the eating of bread and drinking of wine. Think of one event you would like to be reminded of and design something that could help you remember it. For example, a poppy is used to remind people of those who died in war.

Exploring Christian Belief

Christians remember the last meal Jesus had with his friends by taking part in a special meal. This meal is known by many names: Mass, Communion, Eucharist, the Breaking of Bread etc. A small sip of wine is generally drunk and a small piece of bread is eaten to remember that last meal. This is a difficult story for children to understand. With young children introduce the idea of special meals and sharing food together. As they get older the symbolism can be introduced (bread–body, blood–wine). The story has been adapted for children and does not do justice to the full range of theological interpretations of Mass, Communion etc. Teachers may need to make further adjustments to suit their class.

The washing of the disciples' feet involves symbolic use of water. Water here represents cleansing from wrong. Contrast Jesus' status as lord and teacher with his humility.

A Prayer

Just bread, just wine.
The food of the poor.
Since that day no bread has ever been, just bread.
No wine, just wine.
Reminders of his love call out to us,
Even from the supermarket shelves.

The Arrest

At the end of the evening Jesus and his friends went to a quiet garden called Gethsemane to pray. He asked them pray for him, while he went a little distance from them by himself.

Deeply upset, Jesus talked to God until the sweat ran down his face: 'Father, if it's possible find another way for me to save them besides this suffering. Nevertheless if there is no other way I accept it and I will do what you want.'

Jesus went back to the disciples but they were fast asleep. He looked down at them disappointed: 'Couldn't you even pray for one hour? Wake up now. My enemies are here.'

A force of soldiers arrived led by Judas, one of Jesus' disciples. Judas had been paid to betray Jesus. He had been paid the price of a slave, thirty pieces of silver. He walked up to Jesus and gave him the kiss of welcome,

so that the soldiers and the Temple police knew which person to arrest.

All Jesus' friends ran away in case they were caught too. Only Peter tried to stop Jesus being arrested. He took out a sword and chopped off an ear of the servant of the High Priest. Jesus told Peter off very gently. He knew Peter was trying to help but Jesus was not a violent man. He healed the man's ear and said to Peter, 'Those who live by the sword, die by it.'

Jesus was led away and Peter followed the soldiers at a distance so that he could see where they had taken Jesus.

(John 18:1–11; Matthew 26:36–56;
Luke 22:39–53; Mark 14:32–50)

STORIES AND PRAYERS

The First Trial and Peter's Betrayal

Peter secretly followed the soldiers and Jesus to the High Priest's palace. He did not go inside, instead he waited outside in the courtyard.

A woman recognized Peter and asked him if he was a friend of Jesus. Peter was very frightened. 'No,' he said. 'I never knew the man.'

Another servant came up to Peter and she too thought he was one of Jesus' friends. Peter got angry and shouted, 'I've told you once already, I never knew this man you call Jesus.'

Later on a man came up to Peter and recognized him by his Galilean accent. Once again Peter denied ever knowing Jesus then a cock crowed. Peter cried bitterly when he remembered what Jesus had said.

(*Matthew 26:57–58, 69–75;*
Mark 14:53–72; John 18:12–18, 25–27)

Exploring Christian Belief

Talk about Peter's failure in contrast to his boasting at the Last Supper (page 42). Failing can sometimes be a creative experience people learn from. We can look at mistakes we have made and decide to change. Peter learnt from his mistakes. He was later forgiven and he accepted that forgiveness. The message of Christianity is that there is nothing which God cannot forgive.

Activity

Polish Paper Cutting

Cut a simple cockerel shape out of a piece of coloured paper. Mount the cockerel on white paper.

Cut petal shapes of different sizes from paper, coloured magazines or gift-wrap paper. Glue the petals inside the body of the cockerel.

Underneath your cockerel tell the story of Peter.

Good Friday

The Trial and Verdict

Jesus was put on trial in a religious court. The witnesses against Jesus failed to agree, however, so the religious authorities condemned him to death for insulting God by calling himself the Son of God. Jesus was then sent to the Roman governor, Pilate, because the religious court did not have the power to sentence people to death.

At first Jesus refused to speak. Pilate was fascinated by this man who did not seem to be afraid of him. 'Don't you know I have the power to put you to death?' said Pilate. 'They say you claim to be a king. You can die for making statements like that!'

Jesus explained that he was not like a king of this world. He wanted no power, no armies, no land. The Roman Emperor did not have to worry.

Pilate decided Jesus was innocent and was about to let him go when the religious authorities said, 'If you let him go we will tell the Emperor you let go a rebel who claimed to be a king, and you will get into serious trouble.' Pilate was a weak man and frightened of the Emperor, but he did not wish to have an innocent man's death on his conscience.

Outside the same people who five days earlier had welcomed Jesus into Jerusalem now shouted for his death. Pilate tried reasoning with the crowd: 'I always set free someone at this time of year. I will set free Jesus.'

'No,' shouted the crowd. 'We want Barabbas.' Now Barabbas was a robber who was under sentence of death.

'What shall I do with Jesus?' asked Pilate.

'Crucify him!' yelled the people, the same people who had called 'Hosanna'.

Pilate took a bowl of water and washed his hands saying, 'I wash my hands of the whole affair. I am not guilty of this man's blood.' With that Pilate passed the death sentence and sent Jesus out to die.

(John 18:28–19:16; Luke 23:1–5, 13–25; Matthew 27:1–2, 11–26; Mark 15:1–15)

The Mocking

Jesus was whipped, then the soldiers began to mock him. 'You're a funny-looking king,' they laughed. The soldiers spat at him and hit him. They put a cloak on him and twisted a crown from thorns and put it on his head. The soldiers bowed to him and mocked him saying, 'Hail, King of the Jews.'

The heavy cross-beam was placed on Jesus' back and he walked out to the place of execution. Along the way many of his followers wept to see him so broken. He was so weak from the beating that he fell and another man had to carry his cross for him.

At the hill of Calvary he was crucified with two thieves. Over his head was the notice 'The King of the Jews'. One of the thieves taunted him: 'If you're such a great king why don't you get down from that cross and take us down too?'

The other thief told his friend to shut up: 'We are being punished because we did wrong. This man has done nothing wrong.' Then he turned to Jesus and said, 'Remember me, sir, when you do come into your kingdom.'

Jesus smiled at the thief. 'I will, I promise you. Today you will be with me in paradise,' he replied.

Even though he was in pain, Jesus cried out, 'Father, forgive them, they don't know what they are doing.'

The sky darkened, although it was midday. Everything seemed bleak, as if there was no hope. A cry tore the air as Jesus called out in a loud voice, 'My God, My God, why have you forsaken me?' A little later he said, 'It is finished,' and he died.

(Mark 15:16–39; Luke 23:26–49; John 19:17–37; Matthew 27:27–56)

Activity

The Orthodox cross has three horizontal lines. The top one is for the notice that was pinned over Jesus' head. Read the story again to find out what the notice said.

The longest horizontal line represents the beam Jesus was nailed to.

The small slanted line is the foot-rest. It also stands for the two thieves. The side that points down stands for the bad thief. The side that points up stands for the good thief.

Draw an Orthodox cross and write in the meanings of the different lines.

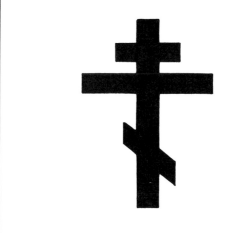

Activity

Make a stained-glass window using tissues and cellophanes. Choose colours which express the sadness of Good Friday.

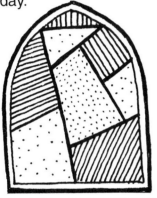

Exploring Christian Belief

Talk about things which make us sad. On Good Friday Jesus' friends felt that everything had gone very wrong. All their hopes were shattered. They had thought Jesus was God's special king but it looked as if they had been wrong. Please emphasize that Good Friday was not the end of the story and handle discussion in such a way that children do not dwell on the torture involved in this story in an unhealthy way. Good Friday is the saddest day of the year for Christians because they remember the lengths Jesus was prepared to go to because of his love. There are various contrasts in this story. Do not try to deal with all of them. Select those which are suitable for your pupils. For example, you could contrast the hatred of the crowd with Jesus' forgiveness or contrast the two thieves. Children could also explore how the Church expresses its sorrow by using black or purple cloth and removing or covering ornaments.

Saturday

On the Friday, before sunset, Jesus had been taken down from the cross and hurriedly buried. He was wrapped in cloth and his body was sealed in a stone tomb. Two guards were put on the door of the tomb because the religious leaders were worried that someone might steal the body and say Jesus had risen from the dead.

On the Saturday, the day after Jesus' death, his friends could do nothing except grieve and wait. For it was the Sabbath, the day of rest for Jews when no work could be done.
(Matthew 27:57–61; Mark 15:42–47; John 19:38–42; Luke 23:50–56)

Think About It

How good are you at waiting? When do you have to wait?

Activity

Write a coathanger poem about waiting. Write the word 'waiting' down the middle of the page in large letters. Your first line must have a 'w' in it. Your second line must contain an 'a' and so on.

Now....
I hate....
. . . . w . . .
. . . . a . .
. . . . i . .
. . . . t . .
. . . . i . .
. . . . n . .
. . . . g . . . .

Exploring Christian Belief

Explain that the Jewish Sabbath runs from sunset to sunset. Jesus' body had to be buried rather quickly on the Friday, before sunset, as this could not be done during the Sabbath. The Sabbath ended at sunset on the Saturday but the women could not go to the tomb in the dark, so they waited until the following morning. This is why Christians say Jesus was in the tomb for three days: part of Friday, all day Saturday and part of Sunday. Talk with the children about the difficulties of waiting and the sorts of things they have to wait for. Bring out the contrast between the intense activity of the previous week and the sudden stillness on the Saturday.

STORIES AND PRAYERS

Easter Sunday

The Resurrection

Mary and the other women got up early to go to Jesus' tomb, taking with them spices and sweet-smelling herbs. As they walked along they wondered how on earth they would roll away the enormous stone that stood in front of the entrance of the tomb. When they arrived they were amazed to find that the stone had already been rolled away and the guards had run off.

A man in white stood at the entrance and said to the women, 'Why do you look for the living amongst the dead? He is not here any more. He is risen!'

The women were overjoyed and they quickly ran back to tell the disciples. Peter and John could hardly believe what the women were saying. It seemed so incredible.

Peter and John ran ahead to check for themselves. When they arrived at the tomb they looked inside. They saw the sheet Jesus had been wrapped in but not Jesus. They hurried back to Jerusalem and told the other disciples what they had seen.

Later Jesus appeared to the disciples when they were together in an upstairs room. Only Thomas was absent.

When the disciples saw Jesus they were terrified, for some of them thought he was a ghost! Jesus quietened their fears. 'Give me something to eat,' he said. 'Ghosts don't eat.'

After Jesus had gone Thomas returned. The disciples excitedly told him all that had happened, but Thomas refused to believe it. 'Unless I touch the wounds myself I will not believe it!' he said.

Several days later Thomas did meet Jesus. 'Come and touch my wounds,' invited Jesus. 'See for yourself that I am alive.'

Thomas did not take up the invitation, instead he knelt and said, 'My Lord and my God.'
(John 20–21; Matthew 28; Mark 16; Luke 24)

Activity

Make a stained-glass window using tissues and cellophanes. Choose colours that describe the feelings of a Christian on Easter Sunday.

STORIES AND PRAYERS

Activity

Churches often make Easter gardens to tell the story of Good Friday and Easter Sunday.

Choose an oblong tray. Place some gravel in the bottom and fill it with earth.

Mark the centre of the tray. Bank up the earth on one side to form a hill and place three crosses on the hill.

Bank up the earth on the other half of the tray into a small mound. Push a piece of cardboard tube into the mound and remove any soil from the inside.

Find a suitable stone that would cover the mouth of the tube, but place it slightly away from the mouth so that people can see that the tomb is empty on the Sunday.

Decorate the tomb side of the garden with flowers and mosses. Leave the cross side bare.

Winding a Background

Take strips of stiff card about 2 cm wide and of various lengths. Stick double-sided tape along both sides of the strips.

Choose different shades of wool which you think represent Easter Sunday. Wind the wool round the strips, leaving no gaps.

Join the strips by fixing them to a piece of strong card using safe glue. Place the board behind the Easter Sunday side of the garden.

Repeat using colours suitable for Good Friday. Place this board behind the Good Friday half of the garden.

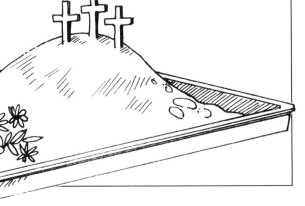

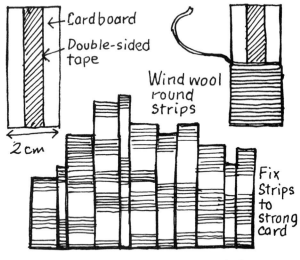

Exploring Christian Belief

Explore the contrasts between Good Friday and Easter Sunday using the two stained-glass windows or the two sides of the garden. Bring out the contrasts between death and life, sorrow and joy.

Note Use a tube from a kitchen roll as this is more hygienic than the centre of a toilet roll.

Assembly Ideas

Run an Easter series using large sheets of paper drawn as a diary. Each day write in the events and tell the appropriate stories. Children can also share the work they have done. For example, they could make large palm crosses to stick on the appropriate page.

Make an Easter garden in assembly. Make a dark background for the Good Friday side. This can be done quickly using drab-coloured hills cut out and glued to purple sugar paper. A contrasting background can be made for the Easter Sunday side. The whole background can be fixed with Blu-Tak to a wall behind the Easter garden.

Prefabricated, very simple, stained-glass windows can be made in assembly from black sugar paper and tissue.

STORIES AND PRAYERS

Newspaper Stories

Look at various newspapers and the style used for headlines. You might like to make a collage of these.

Masked raiders in cash grab

Trouble in the City Centre
Yesterday a group of unemployed youths caused a disturbance in the city centre. They were protesting about the proposed closure of a local youth club and they picketed the Town Hall, making it difficult for workers to get in or out. While the meeting which decided the fate of the youth club was in progress, they kept up a continuous loud chant and handed out leaflets to passers-by.
When interviewed one of the councillors said, 'Although I am sympathetic to their cause, they must understand that tax-payers have to pay for the youth club and we cannot afford to support three youth clubs in this town. Green Hill Youth Club is rather run down. Why should we close one of the better-equipped youth clubs and leave Green Hill open?'

New cadet saves friend's life

Local fire-fighters get Bravery Award

Activity

Local Protesters Make a Stand
Yesterday a group of young people from the Green Hill Youth Club protested outside the Town Hall over the closure of their club. Green Hill Youth Club is in an area of high unemployment. When asked why they were protesting Kerry Townsend, one of the protesters, said, 'There is little to do in our area and few jobs. The youth club is one of the few places where we can go, and it helps keep people out of trouble. We are here to make the council think again because we need a youth club in Green Hill.'
The protest was conducted in a peaceful manner. The members of the club just stood outside the Town Hall chanting and handing leaflets to people who passed by.

Look at the two imaginary newspaper articles. Read the stories carefully then answer these questions:

- What differences between the stories do you notice?
- Are the 'facts' the same or do they conflict?
- Is there a different emphasis in the different newspapers?
- Do the stories seem to be written from a particular point of view?
- Which version of the story did you like best? Why?
- Do the articles help you understand both points of view?
- Whose side would you be on?

Activity

In groups, choose one of the Easter stories.

Divide into two smaller groups. Each smaller group should write an account of the events from a different point of view using a suitable headline. For example:

Popular Preacher Arrested in Garden
(Local newspaper sympathetic to Jesus)

Trouble-maker Seized by Temple Police
(Official newspaper of the religious authorities)

Exploring Christian Belief

Christians believe Jesus was unjustly treated. He was innocent of any crimes against people. The ordinary people loved him. The authorities hated him. To the authorities Jesus was a trouble-maker and a challenge to their position. Many of his followers still are. Oscar Romero (El Salvador) and Janani Luwum (Uganda) both died because they condemned their government for its treatment of the people. People reacted to Jesus in different ways. Bring out these contrasts.

Note Please make it plain that not all the Jews in authority reacted negatively to Jesus. A positive picture of the authorities is painted in Nicodemus, Gamaliel and Joseph of Arimathea. Ordinary Jewish people reacted very positively to Jesus.

WRITING

The Coin, Leaf and Feather

An Imaginary Story

The disciple Peter died in Rome and his young grandson Symeon sat sorting through his grandfather's belongings. In his grandfather's chest he found a small box and inside the box a feather, a leaf and a coin. With the objects was a scroll which told of the events in the last week of Jesus' life.

Symeon took the objects out and placed them on a clean white cloth. He read the scroll and as he read it he tried to imagine what part these objects had played in the story.

Was the coin some of the money Judas was given or was it something else? What was the leaf? What was the feather? Why had his grandfather kept these things?

Activity

Write what you think the coin, leaf and feather were and what part they played in the last week of Jesus' life. Why do you think Peter kept them?

Exploring Christian Belief

The story about Peter's grandson is an imaginary one, but people do keep mementoes of important events, events of great happiness or sadness, and Easter was both of these. Adults may keep pressed flowers from a wedding bouquet, locks of a baby's hair or their first bootees. Ask the children if they have mementoes of holidays or other things they like to remember. They might like to start a mementoes display. We do not know if any of the disciples kept mementoes. If they did they were mementoes not of a past friend, but of a present one, for Easter is the story of Jesus rising from the dead so that he can still be people's invisible friend. Some teachers might like to develop the link with Mass/Communion/Eucharist at this point (see page 103 for further ideas).

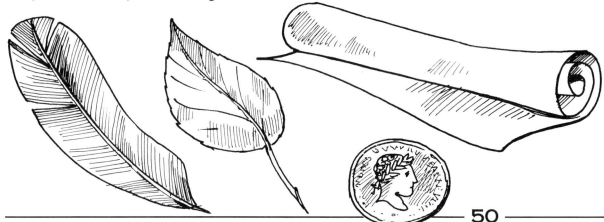

Untold Stories

Activity

Read the story of the first Palm Sunday.

When Jesus entered Jerusalem people broke off branches and laid them down for his donkey to walk over. They also spread out their coats. It was like laying a red carpet.

Imagine some children joining in. How will they explain their messy coats to their mums? What would your family think if you came home with your coat covered in footprints?

Start your story with a child walking home with their coat. What do their parents do? How does the child explain what happened?

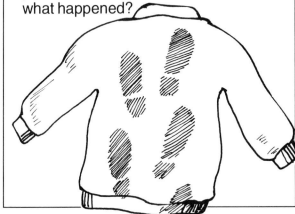

Note The children will need a copy of the story of Palm Sunday (page 38) for this activity.

WRITING

Activity

Read the story of Jesus clearing out the Temple.

Jesus turned over the stalls where people changed money in the Temple courtyard. Imagine you were left in charge of a stall while the owner went for lunch. How will you explain to the owner what happened?

Start your story when the owner comes back and finds a terrible mess. How does he or she react? How do you explain the money being all over the floor?

Note The children will need a copy of the story of Jesus clearing out the Temple (page 40) for this activity.

Assembly Ideas

Rub chalk on some trainers and make footprints on an old anorak. Use this to introduce the story of Palm Sunday. Use the children's stories to illustrate the family's reaction. If possible turn them into sketches.

Encourage the staff to bring in various mementoes and talk about their significance. Take in an artificial feather, a coin, a leaf and a scroll and let the children read their work. Talk about Peter's memories of that week. What would he have wanted to forget?

Bring in a variety of newspapers and read some suitable headlines. Let the children read their accounts from different points of view.

Easter Haikus

Activity

A **haiku** is a poem with three lines. It does not have to rhyme but it does have to have a certain number of beats or syllables:

- Line 1 has **five** beats.
- Line 2 has **seven** beats.
- Line 3 has **five** beats.

A haiku is like a snapshot: it catches one moment in time.

1. Decide on one moment from one of the Easter stories: for example, Peter crying in the courtyard.

2. The first line of your haiku should describe **where** the action took place. For example:

In the darkest corner

3. The next line describes **what** the action was. For example:

Peter wept bitter tears

△ △ △ △ △

O O O O O O O

▢ ▢ ▢ ▢ ▢

4. The last line says **when** the action took place. For example:

Through the long night

5. Now put your lines together. You may need to change your words to get the right number of beats in each line. Do not worry about the beats too much until you have written your poem. You can always alter words afterwards. For example, this poem needs changing:

In the darkest corner (6)
Peter wept bitter tears (6)
Through the long night (4)

Here is one way to make it into a haiku:

In the dark corner (5)
Peter wept bitter salt tears (7)
Through the long, deep night (5)

O O O O O

△ △ △ △ △ △ △

✳ ✳ ✳ ✳ ✳

WRITING   **POETRY**

An Easter Cinquain

A **cinquain** is a poem that has a certain number of words or beats in each line:

- Line 1 has **one** word (the title).
- Line 2 has **two** words.
- Line 3 has **three** words.
- Line 4 has **four** words.
- Line 5 has **one** word (related to the title).

Activity

Write a cinquain about Easter.

1. Write a one-word title as your first line.

Example   Easter

2. Write a two-word line about Easter as your second line.

Example   Chocolate time

3. Write a three-word line about Easter.

Example   Season of joy

4. Write a four-word line about Easter.

Example   The stirring of life

5. Now think of one word describing Easter or repeat your title.

Example   Easter!

6. Put your lines together to complete your cinquain.

Example   Easter.
           Chocolate time,
           Season of joy,
           The stirring of life,
           Easter!

Activity

Write a cinquain on a character or event from one of the Easter stories.

Exploring Christian Belief

Discuss the importance of Easter to Christians and how this is expressed in worship. You might like to invite in Christians from various traditions to share why Easter is important to them.

Note This is an adapted form of the cinquain. A traditional cinquain has twenty-two *syllables:* two in Line 1, four in Line 2, six in Line 3, eight in Line 4, two in Line 5.

Colour Poems

Activity

What colours do you think of as sad colours? Write a poem for Good Friday using sad colours. For example:

Sadness is a grey sky in November
Frozen brown mud
Black ink.

What colours do you think of as joyful colours? Write a poem for Easter Sunday using joyful colours. For example:

Joy is a yellow sun in the school holidays
A red balloon
White ice cream.

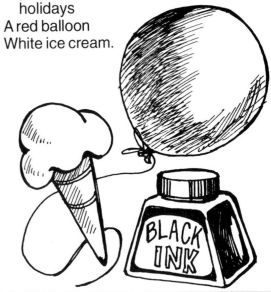

The Song of . . .

There is an old Saxon poem where the cross on which Jesus died speaks and tells its story:

I remember the morning a long time ago when I was cut down,
I was severed from my roots.
Men loaded me on their shoulders and set me on a hill.

Activity

Choose one of the Easter stories. Read it through carefully.

Choose one object from the story. If that object could speak, what would it say?

Write its speech in the form of a poem.

Think About It

What would the song of the road be in the story of the first Palm Sunday? What would the song of the stone be in the story of Jesus rising from the dead?

The Song of the Palm

Waving gentle in the breeze
So warm yet hanging between earth and heaven,
I am free from harm, only I do not see it coming
A time to roar and cry,
I need only hope to keep me alive.
Then a crash
And my whole body shook as I fell to the ground
Then I rise, float and fall on the hard road,
For the donkey to walk on my leaves
And I am forgotten and left to die.

(*Nicky Jo, aged 11,*
Stevenson County Primary School)

The Song of the Palm

Swinging freely through the breeze
Suddenly it happened!
I could sense danger.
Something reaching
High into the tree,
A sharp crack
Running through my spine.

Then slung over the man's shoulder,
Carried away
To a cheering crowd,
Thrown on the road.
There was a shout
'Lord, Lord!'
The crowd made a path,
I saw a man in a white robe,
On a donkey he came.

As the donkey's feet touched me
I felt a tingle of feelings,
Happiness, sadness, fear, sorrow
All of them flowed through me like gold.

(*Shirley, aged 10,*
Stevenson County Primary School)

Exploring Christian Belief

The symbol of the cross is important to Christians; it was on the cross that Jesus died, defeating evil. Christians think of Easter as a victory. There is a point in chess where you know your opponent is defeated but you have not played out all the moves. Easter is a little like that. Christians believe Jesus defeated evil, death and all the power of wrong, but people still experience these. It is as if the battle is not over but the outcome is sure. Good will win.

POETRY

Easter Poems

Palm Sunday

That one day in Jerusalem
a man went riding in
along a welcome path of palms
to celebrate the Passover.

This Saturday in Redditch Centre
shoppers shuttle by
beneath redundant palm leaves
safely out of reach.

That one day hoof and sandal
turned the palm leaves underfoot
to print a welcome message
across two thousand years.

This Saturday no eyes look back
or lift beyond shopwindow height;
and decorative palms
will neither praise them nor condemn.

Today into imagination come
those folded palm leaf crosses
given out in Sunday School.
I pinned them pointing down

the ages back to Calvary.
We should maybe blade them
pointing upward, poised
to scratch a meaning back to life.

(*Barrie Wade*)

Easter

How can he tell
It is the hour
To burst the shell
And overpower
The cold hard prison walls?
It is the Easter wonder!

Into the sun,
The clean fresh air;
His life begun,
He stands to stare,
For Spring is all around.
It is the Easter wonder!

The trees and flowers
Are now new-dressed;
In sunshine hours
The birds build nests.
New life is all around.
It is the Easter wonder!

And from the tomb
Our Lord did rise,
Dispelling gloom;
Gave us the prize
Of everlasting life.
It is the Easter wonder!

(*A. Elliott-Cannon*)

There is a man with back bent in pain,
The weight he bears a heavy cross
As people call and jeer.
Beads of sweat and blood mingle,
And a crown of thorns mocks.
His face a portrait of pain.

The man hangs calm and still
The weight he bears the people's sins
As people cry and weep.
The world is black as night,
But radiance lights his face.
His face is a portrait of peace
For all the world to share.

(*Amy, aged 10,
St Paul's School, Hereford*)

Exploring Christian Belief

These poems can be used in many ways: as a stimulus for writing or art, as a starter for discussion, or just listened to and enjoyed. Explore the symbols used in the poems and their religious significance.

Assembly Ideas

Encourage the children to share their poems. They could also share what is important about Easter for Christians.

Children could bring in objects, fabrics, etc. of various colours for their colour poems.

Start an assembly on the children's 'Song of . . .' poems by asking what various objects might say if they could speak.

Water-bugs and Dragonflies

Activity

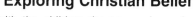

Find out about the life-cycle of the dragonfly. Where will you find this information? Who could help you?

Water-bugs

Roll a piece of thin card into a cylinder shape and fasten it. Tear tissue paper into pieces and glue them to the roll until it is completely covered. What colours will you use?

Make six legs for your water-bug. How will you do this? How are you going to fasten them on?

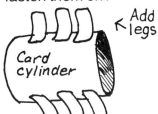

Dragonflies

Take a long drinking-straw and paint the top 10 cm with glue. Wind strips of tissue round the glued part of the straw to make the body of the dragonfly. Look at pictures of dragonflies so that you can decide which colours to use.

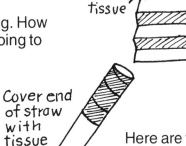

Tissue wings

Pinch

Attach to straw

Pleat tissue

Cover end of straw with tissue

Cut

Place inside cylinder and push up

Here are two ways to make the wings:

- Cut a length of tissue, cellophane or foil as shown. Pinch it in the middle and sellotape it to the straw.

- Fold a length of tissue like a fan. Snip the end of the fan diagonally. Attach it to the straw.

Place the dragonfly inside the water-bug. Push up as shown.

Exploring Christian Belief

Discuss with the children the tremendous changes that take place between water-bugs and dragonflies. The book *Waterbugs and Dragonflies*, by Doris Stickney (Mowbray), sensitively uses this analogy to explain death to children. The story may be summarized as follows:

The water-bugs played happily at the bottom of the pond. Their happiness was occasionally marred when a fellow water-bug left and disappeared above the surface of the pond. They did not know the bug changed into a dragonfly and the dragonfly could not get back to tell them that leaving the pond was not the end.

This story can be applied to Easter rather than death in general. If you do so, you can explain that Christians believe that once someone, Jesus, did come back to reassure people that death was not the end.

Note Make sure all glues used are safe. Check that no child has been recently bereaved and handle very sensitively.

ART

Split Pictures

Wax Pictures

Activity

Divide a piece of paper in two. You can divide it in any way you want.

Draw one of the split pictures suggested below or invent your own subject.

Night to Day

On one side of your picture draw a night scene. On the other draw a picture of the sun.

Seed to Flower

On one side of your picture draw a seed in the earth. On the other draw the flower.

Winter to Spring

On one side of your picture draw a winter scene. On the other draw a spring scene.

Caterpillar to Butterfly

On one side of your picture draw a caterpillar or chrysalis. On the other draw the butterfly.

Egg to Chick

On one side of your picture draw an egg. On the other draw the chick.

Activity

Take a sheet of light-coloured paper and draw a sunrise using wax crayons. Press hard with the wax crayons and use them thickly.

When you have finished your drawing, paint over the whole picture using diluted **dark** water-based paints and a large brush or sponge.

What happens to the picture?

Exploring Christian Belief

Encourage the children to make their split pictures using as many different techniques as possible. These pictures represent ways of looking at death and resurrection. The Easter story contains the same contrasts: the sorrow of Good Friday and the joy of Easter Sunday. The wax picture is a visual way of representing Good Friday/Easter. For a moment the picture disappears and everything looks very black then the picture comes through better than ever.

Topsyturvy People

Activity

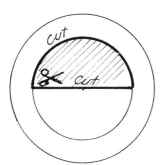

Paper plate

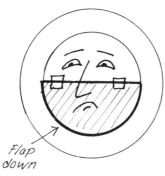

Flap down

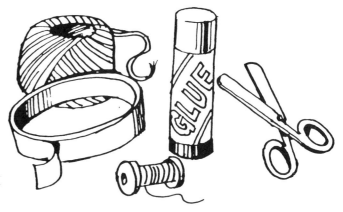

Take a paper plate and cut out the centre circle. Cut the circle in half.

Take another paper plate and draw a line half-way across the middle.

When you have made your hinge, fix your half-circle to your paper plate.

With the extra half-circle at the bottom, draw a sad face.

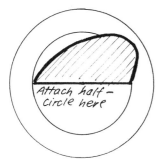

Attach half-circle here

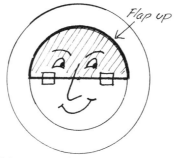

Flap up

Place the half-circle on the centre-line. How can you attach the half-circle so that you can flip it up or down? What could you use as a hinge?

Now fold your half-circle upwards and draw a happy face.

How could you change the expression on the face quickly from sad to happy?

Exploring Christian Belief

Use the topsyturvy people to tell the Easter story. Be careful when doing art on the Easter story. Some children seem to focus on the means of Jesus' death in a rather unhealthy way. If they do want to do something specifically on Good Friday it might help to suggest slightly more abstract art techniques, e.g. shadow-rubbings of a cross (see page 26) rather than detailed pictures. The importance of Good Friday for Christians is *who* died and *why*, not the finer details of how he died.

Assembly Ideas

Use giant versions of the topsyturvy people, the water-bug and dragonfly and the wax pictures. Make them 'Blue Peter' style during the assembly.

ART

Easter Carols

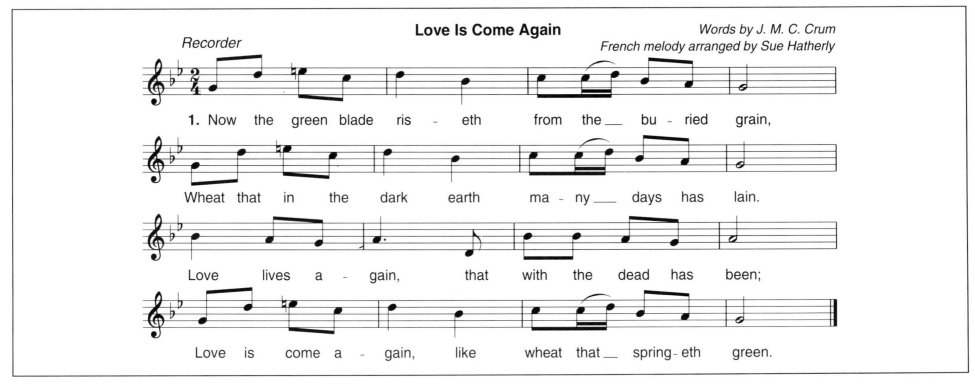

Love Is Come Again

Words by J. M. C. Crum
French melody arranged by Sue Hatherly

Recorder

1. Now the green blade ris - eth from the __ bu - ried grain,

Wheat that in the dark earth ma - ny __ days has lain.

Love lives a - gain, that with the dead has been;

Love is come a - gain, like wheat that __ spring - eth green.

Carols were often accompanied by a circular dance. They were joyous songs of the ordinary people in the Middle Ages. The children might like to make up a circular dance to go with these carols or interpret them in movement.

2. In the grave they laid him, Love whom men had slain.
   Thinking that never he would wake again;
   Laid in the earth like grain that sleeps unseen,
   Love is come again, like wheat that springeth green.

3. Forth he came at Easter, like the risen grain,
   He that for three days in the grave had lain.
   Quick from the dead my risen Lord is seen;
   Love is come again, like wheat that springeth green.

4. When our hearts are wintry, grieving, or in pain,
   Thy touch can call us back to life again.
   Fields of our hearts that dead and bare have been;
   Love is come again, like wheat that springeth green.

Exploring Christian Belief

Nature exhibits continual death and new life. Jesus said that unless a grain of wheat falls to the ground and dies, it cannot live again. The seed has to be buried in order to grow. A bowl of grain is kept in Orthodox churches to remind Christians of the belief that death is not the end, it is the gateway to a new life. The book *Ears and the Secret Song*, by Meryl Doney (Hodder), is based on this carol. It is the story of a harvest mouse whose world is destroyed when the farmer burns the stubble but who sees that world 'resurrected' in the spring.

MUSIC

My Dancing Day

Recorder
Verse

Traditional melody arranged by Sue Hatherly

1. To - mor-row shall be ___ my dan - cing day: I would ___ my true ___ love

did ___ so chance To ___ see the le - gend of ___ my play, To call my

Chorus

true ___ love to ___ the dance: Sing O my ___ love, O ___ my

love, my love, my love; This have I done ___ for my ___ true love.

2. In a manger laid and wrapt I was,
   So very poor, this was my chance,
   Betwixt an ox and a silly poor ass,
   To call my true love to the dance:

3. For thirty years I lived and taught,
   A wandering teacher was my stance.
   I healed the sick, the lost I sought,
   To call my true love to the dance:

4. Then on a cross I hung to die,
   Where a spear to my heart did glance;
   'It is finished' was my cry,
   To call my true love to the dance:

5. Then to the tomb I made my way
   For my true love's deliverance,
   And rose again on the third day
   Up to my true love and the dance:

   (*Adapted*)

Assembly Ideas

If appropriate, share the songs in assembly and encourage the children to perform circular dances (carols) to them.

Use some of the Easter music to introduce assemblies.

Music for Easter

Many composers have written Easter music. Encourage the children to listen to the way different composers have expressed the story of Easter: the horror at the arrest, the sadness of the crucifixion, the joy of the resurrection and the faith that death is not the end of life. For example:

- *Stainer's 'Crucifixion'* Chorus and solo 'The Agony' (the Garden of Gethsemane and arrest); chorus 'God So Loved the World' (love); chorus 'Father, Forgive Them' (forgiveness).

- *Bach's 'St Matthew Passion'* Chorus 'Have Lightnings and Thunders Their Fury Forgotten?' (indignation at the arrest); chorale 'O Sacred Head Sore Wounded' (sadness, the crucifixion); chorus 'In Tears of Grief' (grief, Jesus is buried).

- *Handel's 'Messiah'* 'The Trumpet Shall Sound' (the hope of life after death).

- *Bach's 'St John Passion'* Aria 'O My Troubled Mind' and chorale 'Without Thinking' (both on Peter's denial); chorale 'Who has Hit You Like That?' (Jesus on trial).

- *Marie Keyroux's 'Chant Byzantin. Passion et Résurrection'* Easter Sunday chant 'Christ is Risen' (the joy of the resurrection).

Activity

Make up some Easter music of your own. Make some of it sad and some of it joyful.

Exploring Christian Belief

Christians believe that death is not the end, it is a new beginning. Jesus rising from the dead was the first example of resurrection. Death was not the end for Jesus. Christians believe it is not the end for others either, although they believe they will not see people who die again in this life.

MUSIC

Greetings

Warm-up

Ask the children to walk round the room shaking hands with as many people as possible.

Next ask them to walk round the room in different directions without bumping into each other. Ask them to greet the person nearest them with 'Hello' when you clap. Repeat this so that each time you clap they greet a different person. They are not allowed to greet the same person twice.

Ask the children to walk slowly round the room again. This time when you clap they must greet each other using another form of greeting, not 'Hello'.

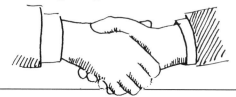

Activity

People from different parts of the world greet each other in different ways. Find out about greetings from various places or cultures and practise greeting each other in these different ways.

Activity

Greetings can be unspoken: a bow, a smile, a hug or a wave. Explore different non-verbal greetings in drama.

Activity

In groups, make up sketches using an imaginary door. One person knocks and walks through the door and the rest of the group either welcome them or make them feel unwelcome.

Make sure each person experiences both a good and a bad welcome.

Remember that you can make people feel welcome or unwelcome by using body language or tone of voice as well as words.

Activity

Read the story of Palm Sunday. Which words and gestures did the crowd use to welcome Jesus? Act out that Palm Sunday welcome.

If Jesus had come to Japan or Great Britain rather than Palestine, how might people have welcomed him?

Act out a Palm Sunday welcome using greetings from a different part of the world.

Note The children will need a copy of the story of Palm Sunday (page 38) for this activity.

Exploring Christian Belief

The entry into Jerusalem (Palm Sunday) was far more than a welcome. It was a royal entrance. Jesus was entering the capital city as its king, but a peaceful king and a king who came to serve. He entered on an ass not a war-horse. That welcome was in sharp contrast to the rejection that happened less than a week later, when the same crowd shouted 'Crucify'.

Note Teachers may prefer to give the instructions for the activities verbally rather than photocopying and handing them out to the children.

DRAMA

Contrasts in Movement

Here are a few suggestions for opposites in movement. You can develop more with the children.

- Level: high/low.
- Tempo: slow/fast.
- Weight: heavy/light.
- Flow: smooth/jerky, flowing/staccato movements.
- Size: large/small body shapes.
- Space: children can occupy space close to them or as far away as they can stretch. They can move through their space in a straight or roundabout fashion.
- Shape: rounded/elongated, symmetrical/asymmetrical.
- Direction: forwards/sideways/backwards.
- Pathway: children can follow a curved pathway, an angular pathway or a zigzag. The pathway can be on the ground or in the air.
- Body parts: head/feet, fingers/toes, arms/legs, knees/elbows.
- Activity: sinking/rising, twisting/straight, advancing/retreating, bending/stretching, open/closed, meeting/parting, still/moving.

Spend time developing the above contrasts with the children. They can then create opposite movements in pairs, one partner performing a movement and the other responding with the opposite movement.

The movements can be accompanied by music. The children can also interpret their movements using musical instruments.

Exploring Christian Belief

The skills built up in the above work can be used in drama on Easter to bring out the contrasts in the story.

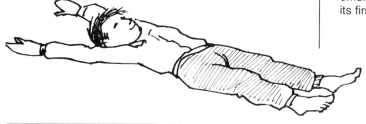

Ways of Understanding

Caterpillars to Butterflies

Start the children off as caterpillars: pulling themselves up and reaching out, curling and stretching, the caterpillars' movements becoming slower and slower until they are completely still.

The children can then make weaving movements as they spin their cocoons. This can be done in spiral movements at different levels.

The children can finally become butterflies slowly breaking out of the cocoon. Try to avoid the children 'flapping' as butterflies. If possible watch a video of a butterfly emerging: the wings crumpled and unfolding, slowly drying; the butterfly making its first hesitant movements and finally gaining confidence in flight.

Water-bugs to Dragonflies

Look at the swimming movements of water-bugs and the very different flight of the dragonfly.

Seed to Flower

Ask the children to imagine a dark damp enclosed seed, tightly bound by the soil. The children can curl up tightly, using as little body space as possible. They can then uncurl as the shoot pushes upwards towards the light and the leaf unfolds.

Egg to Chick

Ask the children to curl up into an egg shape with their limbs packed tightly against each other. Slowly the chick emerges, freeing one part at a time. The chick then takes its first hesitant steps.

Winter to Spring

The children can be:

- Swirling snow
- Sharp frost
- Bare branches caught in the wind
- Frozen puddles
- Blizzards
- Smothering fog

- Spring sunshine
- Soft breezes
- Gentle rain
- Growing plants
- Animals emerging

Day to Night

Move with the children through the day: waking up, breakfast, school, play, etc., until they settle down to sleep again.

Exploring Christian Belief

These are different ways of understanding the Christian belief that life comes out of death, that hope is sometimes born out of despair, that joy sometimes comes after painful experiences. The Bible says that a plant grows only by the seed itself dying. No one worries about the poor little conker when they see the magnificence of the horse-chestnut tree.

Assembly Ideas

Use the sequences which provide different ways of expressing death and resurrection. These can accompany stories from the Stories and Prayers section (pages 44–47).

Use different opposites in movement in a series of assemblies. Follow the movements with stories about opposites (see page 37).

Encourage the children to demonstrate different greetings and tell the story of Palm Sunday (page 38).

DRAMA

Badges

Activity

Think about the sort of person you are. Make a badge which will tell someone else something about you. You could draw something to do with a hobby or something which is important to you.

When you have made your badge, design a safe way to attach it which will not harm your clothes.

When everyone has finished, put all the badges in a bowl and mix them up. Each person should then take out one badge and wear it.

What does the badge you selected tell you about the person who made it? Find the owner and see if you were right.

Think About It

Was it easy to choose one thing to put on a badge to represent you? How many badges would you need to make to give someone a good idea of the sort of person you are?

Activity

Choose one character from the Easter story (not Jesus) and make a badge for them. Draw something on the badge that will say something about that person.

Exploring Christian Belief

Discuss 'labelling' with the children. Badges are like labels. They tell us something about a person, but not everything. Sometimes we stick an invisible label on someone: we call them 'grumpy' or 'cheerful' but we never find out any more about them. People have many sides to their characters. No person can be summed up in a couple of words. The same is true of the characters in the Easter story. Thomas gets labelled as 'Doubting Thomas', Peter is seen as the one who denied Jesus, and Judas as a betrayer. We need to be careful not to stick unhelpful labels on people. Christians and others also need to look at the Bible characters as a whole, not just stick a label on them because of one incident. For example, Thomas was very brave and was also the first person to have enough faith to call Jesus 'My Lord and my God', yet the title 'Doubting Thomas' has stuck!

Easter Around the World

My name is Weiling. I live in Singapore. At the Good Friday evening service no one is allowed to wear colourful clothing. After the service each person is given a lighted candle and we walk round the church singing about the cross of Jesus. A large white cardboard cross which has holes all over it is placed in the aisle. We line up and place posies of flowers in the holes. Soon the cross becomes a cross of flowers.

Some Christians get up very early on Easter morning and have an outdoor service on the beach as the sun rises over the sea.

My name is Nadem. I live in Pakistan. On Good Friday we spend a long time in church. The service lasts three hours and seven short sermons are preached, each lasting five to ten minutes! The sermons are on the seven sayings of Jesus on the cross.

On Easter Sunday morning we get up at 4 a.m. and walk through the village with lighted candles, singing and playing musical instruments. We have an early morning service and then we have breakfast together.

My name is Crisanta. I live in the Philippines. On Good Friday when we go to church there is a life-size statue of Jesus in a glass coffin on display. Good Friday is a very sad day. We remember that Jesus suffered for us. We have to behave ourselves on Good Friday. No one is allowed to shout or laugh out loud.

Hello, I'm Shanta. I live in South India. On Good Friday we wear white to church and we eat a sour chutney with our rice to remind us of Jesus' suffering. On Easter Sunday everybody wears their best clothes and the church is decorated with flowers such as white lilies and chrysanthemums.

PAST/PRESENT

Activity

Explore other Easter customs which bring out the contrast between Good Friday and Easter Sunday.

Exploring Christian Belief

Talk about the beliefs which lie behind these different practices. Children might like to design their own service for a group of Christians, devising appropriate ways of expressing grief (Good Friday) and joy (Easter Sunday). In some schools it may be appropriate to make a cardboard cross and fill it with flowers. A link could be made between the sour chutney and the bitter herbs used by Jews in the Passover meal. More information on Easter customs and Easter food around the world can be found in *Feasting for Festivals,* by J. Wilson (Lion), and *When Christians Meet* (CEM).

Assembly Ideas

Run a series of assemblies on Easter around the world. Each day take a different country, look at its geographical position and share some basic information about it. Finish with how Christians in that country celebrate Easter.

Cross-curricular Links

Easter Flowers

Children might like to investigate the meaning of the passion-flower. The word 'passion' (deep feeling) is used to describe Jesus' death. Each part of the passion-flower has a different meaning:

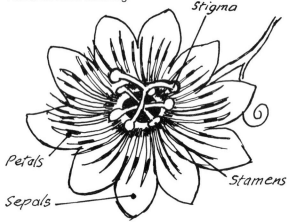

- The three lobed stigma stand for the nails.
- The five stamens below them stand for the five wounds/scars.
- The spiky circle of petals represents the crown of thorns.
- The ten sepals stand for the ten disciples not counting Judas and Peter, who were disloyal.

White lilies are used in churches at Easter. They symbolize mourning and innocence. On Easter Sunday white and yellow flowers are used. The children might like to plant suitable flowers of those colours. Please check all plants for safety.

Geography

Children can look at general contrasts such as hot and cold lands, wet areas and deserts, mountains and plains, barren and fruitful areas, land and sea, opposite points of the compass.

Science

Children can contrast hot and cold, light and heavy, sinking and floating, solids and gases, good conductors of heat and poor conductors, good conductors of electricity and poor conductors, pushing and pulling, attraction and repulsion (magnets).

Technology

The properties of different materials can be contrasted and how this would affect their use: bendy/rigid, waterproof/not waterproof, smooth/rough, static and moving objects.

Maths

Multiplication and division, addition and subtraction are arithmetical opposites. Children can also look at contrasts and opposites in shape and arrange objects in sets with contrasting properties: rounded/angular, symmetrical/asymmetrical, odd/even (sides or faces), long/short, big/small, flat/solid, straight/curved.

Useful Books

The Lion, the Witch and the Wardrobe, by C. S. Lewis (Puffin).
Pangur Ban, by Fay Sampson (Lion).
Donkey's Day Out, by A. Pilling (Lion).
The Surprise Present, by E. Brown (Lion).
Haffertee's First Easter, by J. and J. Perkins (Lion).
Waterbugs and Dragonflies, by D. Stickney (Mowbray).
The Lion Easter Book, by M. Batchelor (Lion).
The Easter Book, by A. Farncombe (NCEC).
Ears and the Secret Song, by M. Doney (Hodder).
Projects for Easter, by G. Cooke (Wayland).
Easter Words, by P. Eagan (Church House Publishing). A good selection of prayers, poems and sections of novels on Easter themes such as suffering, love, sacrifice, death and resurrection.

Orange Rolling

On Dunstable downs on Easter Sunday you will find people rolling oranges. Maybe this reminds them of the stone being rolled away from the tomb of Jesus.

Activity

Try rolling your own oranges down a plank. How steep does the plank have to be before the orange will roll if it is held at the top and released, not pushed?

How can you measure the angle?

Egg Cracking

In Orthodox churches eggs are dyed bright red to remind people of Jesus' death. On Easter morning the eggs are tapped against each other, rather like the game of conkers. When an egg cracks it reminds people of Jesus breaking out of the tomb and rising from the dead.

Activity

Try dying your own hard-boiled eggs red by adding natural food colouring to the water.

Russian Christians draw a special cross on the front. You can do this with special cake-decorating pens or you can make a cross pattern in wax on your egg before you dye it.

Note Make sure all eggs are boiled until hard and only safe food colours are used.

Assembly Ideas

Demonstrate these games in assembly explaining the meaning behind them.

Quick Hot Cross Buns

Activity

These buns are traditionally eaten for Good Friday breakfast. The cross is a symbol of Jesus' death.

You will need

450 g strong white flour
1 level teaspoon salt
1 level teaspoon mixed spice
50 g margarine
50 g caster sugar
1 packet easy-blend yeast
175 g currants
50 g sultanas
1 beaten egg
250 ml warm milk
a little oil
pastry for the crosses
milk and sugar for glazing

heatproof mixing-bowl
wooden spoon
baking-trays
large polythene bags
rolling-pin
knife
pastry-brush
wire racks

Method

Ask an adult to set the oven to gas mark 2/150°C (300°F).

1. Measure the flour, salt and spice into a heatproof bowl and put them in the oven to warm for about 3 minutes.

2. Rub in the margarine. Add the sugar, yeast and fruit and stir well.

3. Add the egg and warm milk and mix well. Knead until smooth

4. Cut the dough into four pieces. Cut each quarter into six or eight and shape into buns.

5. Place on greased and floured baking-trays.

6. Put inside oiled polythene bags. To oil a bag, put in a dessertspoonful of oil and shake well.

7. Leave in a warm place until the buns double in size.

8. Ask an adult to turn up the oven to gas mark 6/200°C (400°F).

9. While the buns are rising make the crosses. Roll out a small amount of pastry and cut it into strips. Most people put a simple Greek cross on their hot cross buns but you could use other types: for example, a Latin, Maltese or Celtic cross.

10. When the buns have risen, place the strips of pastry on top and glaze the buns with sugar and milk (1 tablespoon of sugar to 5 tablespoons of warm milk). If the crosses do not stick well, brush underneath them with milk.

11. Bake for about 15 minutes until the buns sound hollow when tapped underneath. Cool on wire racks.

Note   Different crosses can be found on page 25.

COOKING

Easter Bread

Activity

Use a simple bread recipe to make Easter bread from the following countries. Shape the dough and add all decorations before you allow the dough to rise.

Crete

Arrange some of the dough in a circle. Make dough flowers and leaves to decorate it. Stick them on with a little milk.

Norway

Roll the dough into 'sausages'. Tie each sausage into a loose knot. Make one end the tail of a chick and one end the head. Use a currant for the eye:

Greece

Hard boil an egg in water tinted with natural red food dye. Make a plait of dough. When the egg is cool place it in the centre of the plait.

Do not eat the egg as it will be rather overcooked and rubbery.

Think About It

What beliefs do these different breads express?

Note There is a basic bread recipe in *Christianity Topic Book 1*, pages 62–63. Easter food from many cultures can be found in *Feasting for Festivals*, by J. Wilson (Lion).

Assembly Ideas

Take the various breads into assembly and explain the symbolism. The chick represents new life. The red egg represents the blood of Jesus and his tomb.

Take the hot cross buns into assembly and explain the various crosses.

COOKING

		Page	English	Maths	Science	Technology
Stories and Prayers	Jesus the Teacher	70	1, 2, 3			
	Jesus the Story-teller	71	2, 3			
	Jesus' Message: The Kingdom of God	72	1, 2, 3			1, 2, 3, 4
	Jesus the Powerful	73	1, 2			
	Titles of Jesus	74	1, 2, 3	1, 4		
	Jesus the Friend	76	1			
	Followers of Jesus	76	1, 2			
Writing	The Great Feast	78	1, 2, 3			
	Putting Flesh on Bare Bones	78	1			
	To Preach the Good News	79	1, 2, 3			
Poetry	The Fish	80	2, 3			
	Men Like Trees Walking	80	2, 3			
	I Am	81	1, 3			
	Kennings	81	1, 3			
Art	A Story Frieze: The Lost Sheep	82	1, 2, 3			1, 2, 3, 4
	Symbols of Jesus	83	1			1, 2, 3, 4
	Jesus in Art	84	1, 2			
Music	Songs About Jesus	85	1, 2, 3			
	Music from History	86	1, 2, 3			
Drama	Who Am I?	86	1			
	Jesus' Job	87	1			
	Shadow Puppets	88	1, 2, 3			
PSE	Leaders	89	1, 3			
Past/Present	Names for Jesus	90	1, 2			
Cross-curricular links	History	91	1, 2, 3			
	Citizenship	91	1, 2, 3			
	Technology	91	1, 2, 3	4	3, 4	1, 2, 3, 4
	Geography	91	1, 2, 3		5	5
	Fiction	91	2			
Games	A Christian Puzzle	92	1, 2, 3	1, 2, 3		
Cooking	Gingerbread Men	93	1, 2	1, 2	3	1, 2, 3, 4

NATIONAL CURRICULUM KEY

Attainment Targets	English
1	Speaking and listening
2	Reading
3	Writing
4	Spelling
5	Handwriting
4/5	Presentation

	Maths
1	Using and applying maths
2	Number
3	Algebra
4	Shape and space
5	Handling data

	Science
1	Scientific investigation
2	Life and living processes
3	Materials and their properties
4	Physical processes

	Technology
1	Identifying needs and opportunities
2	Generating a design
3	Planning and making
4	Evaluating
5	Information Technology capability

JESUS

UNDERSTANDING
CHRISTIAN CONCEPTS ABOUT
JESUS

1. It is Jesus who gives Christianity its uniqueness. Who he was (and is) is of vital importance to Christians. Christians believe him to be the Son of God, that he was more than just a good man.

2. Jesus is seen as the second person of the Trinity. This is a difficult idea to explain. Just as water comes in three different forms (water, ice, steam), so God comes in three different forms: God the Father, creator and sustainer of the world; God the Son, the one who became part of that world, lived as a man and experienced human life; God the Holy Spirit, or God in action, God the invisible friend. (The idea of God the Holy Spirit is explored in the topic 'Wind, Fire, Water, Birthday of the Church' in *Christianity Topic Book 2*.)

3. The teachings of Jesus cannot be separated from the rest of his work, or his claims about who he was. In John's gospel the feeding of the five thousand is followed by the sermon in which Jesus calls himself the bread of life.

   Only a small amount of Jesus' teachings is explored in this topic. Teachers will find more examples in other topics in this book and in *Christianity Topic Books 1 and 2*.

4. The Bible depicts Jesus as the healer of broken bodies, broken minds and broken relationships. Various healing miracles are included in this topic. Teachers are referred to the topic 'Reconciliation or Mending Friendships' for examples of Jesus healing broken friendships.

5. Healing people's minds, bodies and friendships was part of Jesus' work to put right those things which spoil the world. Miracles were also seen as signs that Jesus was someone special. Christians believe they were pointers to who he was (and is). Miracles carry a message for Christians, however they are interpreted.

   It is vital when handling healing miracles to make sure that illness and wrong are not associated in a direct sense. Jesus specifically denied that illness or disability is a result of or punishment for sin. Christians believe illness is part of an imperfect world, a world that is not as God intended it to be.

6. Jesus did not perform 'stunts'. He refused to use miracles to stun people into believing in him. He often told people to keep quiet about his healing, and he usually asked for faith on the part of the person being healed or a member of their family. This meant the healing was performed within a relationship rather than for publicity.

7. Jesus was derided as the friend of sinners. He was the friend of people whom society rejected or who had low status: the poor, the sick, the outcasts, the sinful, the young, women and foreigners. Jesus could equally accept invitations to wealthy homes without feeling uncomfortable. He treated everyone as important.

   More information on this aspect can be found in the topic 'Me, My Family and Friends' in *Christianity Topic Book 2*.

8. The titles of Jesus reveal a lot about who Jesus claimed to be and what Christians believe about him. Some of the most important are:

   - *Son of God* Jesus did not use this title very often. When he did it tended to be privately with his disciples. It was this title that finally earned him the death sentence for blasphemy.
   - *Son of Man* This is the title Jesus tended to use. It was a little-known title applied to the Messiah (special king) the Jews were expecting. By using a little-known title Jesus could give it his own stamp, for he was an unusual king who was born in poverty and achieved his ends by suffering. By using the title 'Son of Man' he was also stressing his humanity.
   - *Christ* This is the title for Jesus which most people would recognize. It is just the Greek word for 'Messiah'. Christians believe Jesus was that special, long-awaited king. Throughout this topic Jesus is referred to by name (Jesus) rather than by title (Christ) as his identity can be a sensitive issue for Jews and Muslims.

Jesus the Teacher

Jesus was a very famous teacher. His teachings have lasted nearly two thousand years. Do you think your teacher will still be remembered in two thousand years' time?

Jesus did not just list facts. He taught people using stories such as the story of the Lost Sheep. He used everyday objects and events such as a lost coin (Luke 15:8–10) and a sower (Mark 4:1–20) to help people understand.

He also had a sense of humour. He made jokes about swallowing camels and camels trying to get through the eye of a needle.

Activity

What do you think makes a good teacher? Write a recipe for a teacher. Ask your teacher to do the same.

Show the recipes to teachers and pupils and see if they agree. They might want to add extra ingredients.

Think About It

Would you like to be a teacher?

Jesus' Teaching

Here are two examples of Jesus' teaching.

Plants and Fruit

People do not pick grapes from thornbushes, or figs from thistles. A good tree bears good fruit, but bad trees bear bad fruit. People are like trees: by their fruits (what they do) you will know what sort of people they are. (*Luke 6:43–45*)

Yes and No

Some people use all sorts of oaths when they are speaking. They swear by heaven or earth to make people believe them. Do not swear. Just keep your promises. Make sure your 'Yes' means 'Yes' and your 'No' means 'No'. (*Matthew 5:33–37*)

Activity

Draw some weeds with fruit on them to illustrate Jesus' teaching about plants and fruit.

Prayer

You were the great teacher, unafraid to teach,
Even if what you said was not what people wanted to hear.
Give me the courage to speak what needs saying. Even if it is not popular.

Exploring Christian Belief

Explain that 'fruits' stands for 'actions'. The fruit is the result of the inside life of the plant. Actions are the result of the inside life of a person. Fruits or actions reflect the state of a person's heart. Discuss how the children try to make people believe them by saying 'Honest', 'Cross my heart' etc. Jesus taught uncompromising honesty.

STORIES AND PRAYERS

Jesus the Story-teller

The Lost Sheep

Once there was a shepherd who had a hundred sheep. Each night he brought them into the safety of the sheepfold and counted them to make sure they were all there.

One night he counted the sheep and there were only ninety-nine. He counted them again to make sure, but there was definitely one missing. The shepherd secured the ninety-nine sheep and went out to look for the lost one.

He walked across the hills and through the valley. He climbed the rough paths and he waded through streams until he found the lost sheep. Carefully he placed the sheep on his shoulders and took it home.

He was so glad to have his sheep back that when he reached home he called on all his neighbours and asked them to celebrate with him.   (*Luke 15:3–7*)

Think About It

If you had been the shepherd would you have bothered to search for one sheep? Remember that in Israel there were wild places where wolves, bears and lions still lived.

Activity

The shepherd below is trying to make up his mind whether to go and look for one lost sheep or not. Fill in his thoughts.

Shall I ?

Shan't I ?

Jesus' Stories

Jesus told many stories. Here are some examples:

- The Houses on Rock and Sand (Matthew 7:24–27)
- The Sower (Matthew 13:3–8)
- The Unforgiving Servant (Matthew 18: 23–34)
- The Talents (Matthew 25:14–30)
- The Sheep and the Goats (Matthew 25: 31–46)
- The Good Samaritan (Luke 10:25–37)
- The Rich Fool (Luke 12:16–21)
- The Lost Coin (Luke 15:8–10)
- The Prodigal Son (Luke 15:11–32)
- The Two Sons (Matthew 21:28–31)

Activity

Jesus used stories to teach people something important. Choose one story from the list to read. What do you think Jesus was trying to tell his listeners?

Exploring Christian Belief

Jesus did not tell stories just for entertainment. His stories had a point. Discuss with the children the main points of some of the stories. Encourage them to suggest a variety of interpretations. Children might like to ask some Christians how they interpret the story.

Note Use a children's version of the Bible suitable for the age group you teach. The Palm Tree Bible (Palm Tree Press) is suitable for young children and also comes as separate stories.

STORIES AND PRAYERS

Jesus' Message: The Kingdom of God

For three years Jesus announced his message. He said that God is like a king who invites people to join his kingdom and accept him as their king.

In the story of the Great Feast, Jesus explained that God invites anyone to join his kingdom. It is like being invited to a very important party.

The Great Feast

Once a king held a great feast. He had already sent out all the invitations, so when the party was all prepared he sent his servants to tell the guests that everything was ready. The guests, however, began to make excuses.

Invitation to a party

Please reply

The first one said, 'I can't come. I've just bought a new field and I have to get it ready for ploughing.'

The second one said, 'I'm sorry, I can't come. I've just bought some new oxen and I have to try them out.'

The third one said, 'I can't come. I've just got married.'

The king was very cross when he heard this so he said to his servant, 'Go quickly into the town and bring in the poor and the disabled beggars and those people no one ever invites to a party. They can come to my feast.'

The servant did as his master said but there was still plenty of room and lots of food left over. The king looked around. 'Go into the country,' he said. 'Bring people from the lanes and the fields until my house is completely full!'

(*Luke 14:15–24; Matthew 22:1–14*)

Activity

Design an invitation to a party. Make sure it has a reply slip. On the reply slip write an excuse for **not** coming to the party.

The Kingdom Starts Small

Jesus explained that the Kingdom of God starts as small as a mustard seed. Just as the tiny seed grows into a great bush, so the Kingdom of God grows as more people accept God as their invisible king.

(*Mark 4:30–32*)

Read Matthew 13:33 in the Bible to find out what else Jesus said the Kingdom of God is like.

Entering the Kingdom

Jesus said that entering the Kingdom of God is worth more than anything else. Read the story of the precious pearl (Matthew 13:45–46).

Think About It

Think of your most precious possession. What would you be willing to swop for it? The merchant thought the pearl was so valuable that he swopped everything he had for it.

Exploring Christian Belief

In his *Chronicles of Narnia*, C. S. Lewis describes a land that children enter through a wardrobe. It is the land of the lion Aslan, the great king. The children meet the lion and serve under him. They try to live as the lion wants them to. Even when they are back in England they are still followers of Aslan, still members of Aslan's kingdom even though they no longer live in Narnia. It is like that for Christians. Wherever they live they are followers of Jesus the King. They all belong to the same invisible kingdom, the Kingdom of God.

Jesus the Powerful

The Blind Man at Bethsaida

As Jesus was going through Bethsaida a blind man asked Jesus to heal him. Jesus placed his hands on the blind man's eyes for a moment then asked him if he could see anything.

The man looked up. 'I see men,' he said. 'They look a bit like trees walking.' Jesus covered the man's eyes once more. This time when the man looked up he could see clearly. *(Mark 8:22–26)*

The Wedding at Cana

Jesus went with his mother and friends to a wedding in the town of Cana. The wedding went well but half way through the celebrations the wine ran out.

The host of the party was embarrassed. Mary told Jesus what had happened and told the host to do whatever he said. Jesus was reluctant to do anything publicly but he told the host to fill large jars with water. The host did as Jesus said and when he sipped the water it tasted of the most delicious wine!

People were surprised when they tasted the wine. Normally a host would serve the best wine first and save the worst wine till last. *(John 2:1–11)*

The Roman Centurion's Servant

A Roman soldier who lived in Israel had a servant who was seriously ill. The soldier loved the servant and desperately wanted him to recover, but he knew it was hopeless, his servant was very close to death.

This Roman soldier was very well thought of by the Jews, even though he was an enemy, for he loved God. When he heard about Jesus, he asked his Jewish friends to go to Jesus and ask him to heal his servant. Gladly his friends went and explained the situation:

'Please come and help this man. He is a friend of our nation and loves God. If anyone deserves your help he does!'

Jesus went willingly to the centurion's house. Before he arrived, though, he was stopped by some more friends who passed on a message from the soldier:

'Please don't trouble yourself by coming any further, for I am not good enough to have you under my roof. Just say the word and I know my servant will be healed. I am a man with authority. If I say to my servants "Come!" they come. If I say "Do this!" they do it.'

When he heard this Jesus was amazed. 'I have never met such faith in the whole of Israel,' he exclaimed.

The centurion's friends left. When they reached the house they found the servant well. *(Luke 7:1–10)*

Activity

Who are the powerful people today? Cut out pictures from newspapers and magazines and make a display of powerful people.

Exploring Christian Belief

Children will often ask, 'Why doesn't God work miracles now?' Many Christians would answer that he still does. Not everyone is cured, however, neither did Jesus cure every sick person in Palestine. Illness is seen by Christians as part of a world that has generally gone wrong; it is not as God intended. In no way should illness be linked to sin. Jesus specifically denied this. The biblical vision of the future includes a world where there will be no more crying or pain, no illness. Christians believe that until that day everything possible must be done to put right all that can be. The intelligence that God gave people must be used for positive purposes.

Note The Bible paints a picture of Jesus as powerful. He is seen as having power over disease and the forces of nature. Several healing miracles are retold here but only one nature miracle. The stories of the Feeding of the Five Thousand and the Stilling of the Storm can be found in *Christianity Topic Book 1*, pages 14 and 96. It is usually on the nature miracles that people differ over interpretation.

Titles of Jesus

Son of Man

Jesus experienced what it was like to live a fully human life, with one important difference. Christians believe he never did anything wrong.

This title also means 'judge', a person who judges between right and wrong.

The Life

Jesus said he was 'The Life'. That means he came to help people start a new life with God as their friend. He came to give them a life that even death could not destroy.

The Word

Christians call Jesus 'The Word' because he told people what God is like, what God feels and thinks. The words we say get information from our brain to another person's brain. In the same way Jesus is like a word that tells people about God.

The Door

Jesus said he was like a door that always says 'Come in'. If your mum or dad is in one room and you are in another, you reach them by going through a door. Jesus called himself a door because he helps people to meet God, their heavenly Father.

The Christ

This title means 'special king'. The title 'Messiah' means the same.

The Bread of Life

Just as bread gives people the strength to live, so Jesus gives them strength to live as God's friends.

Alpha and Omega

These are the first and last letters of the Greek alphabet. Christians call Jesus 'Alpha and Omega' because they believe he is the beginning and end of everything, the A to Z.

Immanuel

This word means 'God with us'. Christians believe Jesus is God's son and came to live on earth with human beings.

Saviour

The name Jesus means 'rescuer' or 'saviour'. A saviour is someone who saves people from danger or keeps them safe. Have you ever been in a situation where you needed to be saved or rescued? Christians believe Jesus saves people from the dangers of wrong.

Son of God

Christians believe Jesus was extra special. They believe he was and is God's son.

The Vine

Branches of a vine have to stay attached to the main plant. Christians believe they need to stay close to Jesus.

STORIES AND PRAYERS

The Good Shepherd

Jesus called himself a good shepherd: someone who looks after the sheep and is prepared to die to save them from danger.

The Way

Jesus also described himself as 'The Way'. If you are lost someone might give you directions on how to find the way or they might show you the way. Jesus is like a guide who shows people the way through life and the way to become a friend of God.

King of Kings

The Bible describes Jesus as 'King of Kings'. That means he is a king greater than all kings.

The Light of the World

A light shows up dirt or lights the road so that we can see where we are going. Jesus is described as a light which shows up wrong and shows people the way to go in life.

Lord

When Christians call Jesus 'Lord', they are calling him their ruler. Who rules your country?

The Truth

Christians believe Jesus told the truth about God. Also, if people look at Jesus they can see what God is like. His life told the truth about God.

Prince of Peace

Jesus is not the prince of a place on earth, like the Prince of Wales. He is a ruler who brings peace.

The title 'Prince' can also mean 'son of a king or queen', like Prince Andrew. Christians believe Jesus is God's son.

The Servant

Long ago the Hebrew prophets wrote about a servant of God who would come. Christians believe Jesus was that servant. During his life on earth he behaved like a servant. He came to serve others, not to be served.

Activity

These titles describe Jesus in different ways. Each describes a different 'side' of his character.

Make a multi-faced three-dimensional shape in maths. Write a different title of Jesus on each face, or draw different pictures to illustrate some of his titles.

Activity

Find out what a shepherd's job was like in the first century. Why do you think Jesus called himself a good shepherd?

Exploring Christian Belief

Explain to the children the difference between a title and a name. Explore as many of these titles as is appropriate for your class. You will find activities on them in other sections. For more detailed explanations of each title see *Assemblies for Primary Schools. Summer Term*, by M. Cooling (RMEP).

STORIES AND PRAYERS

Jesus the Friend

Children (Mark 10:13–16)

The poor and the sick (Luke 18:35–41)

People who had done wrong (Luke 19:1–9)

Women (Luke 10:38–41)

Romans – the enemy (Luke 7:1–10)

Exploring Christian Belief

The stories referred to above will need to be read from a children's Bible or put in simple language. Detailed material on Jesus the friend can be found in the topic 'Me, My Family and Friends' in *Christianity Topic Book 2*. Jesus is described in the Bible as the friend of the rejected. When Jesus mixed with the outcasts of society it shocked people. Jesus replied that he was like a doctor: doctors go where they are needed. The more wrong a person had done, the more they needed Jesus.

Followers of Jesus

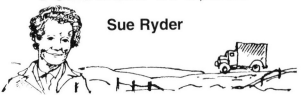

Sue Ryder

Sue Ryder was born and brought up in an English village. Her parents were Christians and Sue had a strong Christian faith of her own. She loved the quiet country life but all that came to an end in 1939, when Britain found herself at war.

Although she was only a teenager Sue joined an organization that helped secret agents. She acted as the agent's driver, did the maintenance on the car and coded the messages.

Later Sue was posted overseas to war-torn Europe attached to the Special Operations Branch. Special Operations dropped agents behind enemy lines. The agents blew up railway bridges, cut telephone wires and generally made things as difficult for the enemy as possible.

Sue was horrified by the suffering she saw in Europe and was determined to do something about it. After the war Sue stayed in Europe and drove five-ton trucks carrying food and medical supplies. She visited the prisoners and she looked after the sick.

STORIES AND PRAYERS

Eventually she set up the Sue Ryder Foundation to help people in need in Britain and abroad. The Foundation runs various homes and centres. It has care teams and mobile medical teams.

Today, long after the war, Sue Ryder's Foundation is still offering care in a world of need.

Activity

You may have heard of Sue Ryder through the many charity shops the Foundation runs. Find out if there is a Sue Ryder shop in your area.

Note The story of Sue Ryder is told in the Faith in Action series under the title *A Living Memorial*, by Audrey Constant (RMEP). See other books in this series for further examples of people who devoted their lives to caring for others.

C. S. Lewis

Clive Staples Lewis was born in Belfast in Northern Ireland in 1898. Although his name was Clive he was always known as Jack. His mother died when he was very young and he was very lonely, particularly when his brother Warnie went away to boarding-school.

When Jack was young he was allowed the run of the house, which was packed with books, and he read anything that interested him. Jack was a lonely boy but he had a good imagination. Soon he began writing stories about an imaginary land inhabited by talking animals. All this came to an end, however, when Jack too was sent to school in England.

Jack was thoroughly miserable. One of his headteachers was extremely cruel and Jack suffered terribly at school. He begged to be taken away. Several years later Jack had his way and was allowed a home tutor instead.

Jack was very clever and went to Oxford University. He did extremely well and was eventually made a tutor.

For many years Jack did not believe in God but slowly he began to change his mind. Eventually he decided that God did exist and that he would become a Christian.

Once Jack had made up his mind there was no stopping him. He used his powerful brain and good imagination to serve God. Jack wrote plays, poetry, radio programmes and all sorts of books about Christianity. He wrote difficult books for adults, he wrote science fiction and he wrote children's books.

His children's books about the magical country of Narnia and the great lion Aslan are very well known. They have been turned into cartoons, plays and television series. The best-known story is *The Lion, the Witch and the Wardrobe.*

Think About It

Think about the things you are good at. How could you use your talents for things that matter to you?

Activity

In the Narnia books Jesus is represented by the lion Aslan. Why do you think C. S. Lewis chose a lion?

Find out a little about Aslan from the books or tapes or videos of the books. Find out the titles of all the Narnia books.

Exploring Christian Belief

Talk with the children about Lewis' life and how he used his talents to share his faith. Many videos and tapes of the Narnia stories are available. Some are abridged for younger children. If children like the Narnia stories they can turn this into a Narnia mini-project and create maps, food, masks etc. Brian Sibley gives lots of ideas for this in *The Magical World of Narnia* (Lions). This book also includes ideas for a Narnia party, which is a good alternative to a Hallowe'en party. Select those activities suitable for your children.

Assembly Ideas

Various series can be run: for example, one on stories about Jesus; one on followers of Jesus; one on stories about the Kingdom of God.

The Great Feast

Activity

Read the story of the Great Feast.

Jesus said that entering God's kingdom is like being invited to a wonderful party.

Look at the party menu card and fill in what you think there was to eat. Decorate your menu.

Think about someone from whom you would really like a party invitation. Describe how you would feel if that invitation arrived.

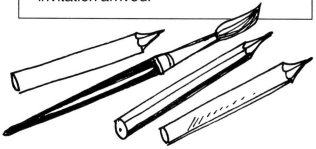

Exploring Christian Belief

Talk with the children about parties and why we have them. Discuss the types of things we celebrate. Explain what is meant by entering the Kingdom of God: it is joining God's family, accepting God as ruler and king. Jesus tried to explain that joining this kingdom is a joyous occasion. It is something to celebrate. It is like being invited to a party by the king. Jesus described it as a party to which everyone is invited, even those society sometimes rejects.

Note The children will need a copy of the story of the Great Feast (page 72) for this activity.

Menu

Putting Flesh on Bare Bones

Activity

Jesus told many stories. Here is one about buried treasure.

The Treasure in the Field

Once a man was digging in a field and discovered a chest which contained tremendously valuable treasure. He quickly filled in the hole, burying the treasure again, and sold everything that he possessed to buy the field. Once he owned the field he could dig up the treasure when he wanted to, and it would all belong to him.

This is only the 'bare bones' of the story. Add details to make the story more interesting for young children but be careful to keep the meaning the same.

Example As the day wore on the sun got hotter and hotter. The sweat dripped from his forehead and ran into his eyes but still he carried on digging.

WRITING

Activity

Organize a treasure hunt for younger children in the school. When they have found the 'treasure', tell them your story of the Treasure in the Field.

How easy do you find story-telling? Is it as easy as it seems?

Exploring Christian Belief

Talk about stories with meanings. Tell a variety of such stories: for example, Aesop's fables and modern stories which carry a message. Discuss with the children stories that have helped them or influenced them. For Christians Jesus' stories are special. Christians believe these stories help them to understand what God is like and how they should live. Discuss with the children what they think the story of the Treasure in the Field means.

Note Jesus told another story very similar to this, often called 'The Pearl of Great Price' (Matthew 13:45–46). An excellent version of this is *The Precious Pearl*, by N. Butterworth and M. Inkpen (Marshall Pickering). Read the biblical version of the story followed by *The Precious Pearl*. This is a splendid example of putting flesh on bare bones.

To Preach the Good News

Jesus said that he had come to tell people about the good news. Often in newspapers we read only the bad news.

Activity

Look through some newspapers and cut out some bad news headlines. Make a display of them.

Now go through the newspapers and find good news. Make a display of good news headlines.

Interview different people about the good things that have happened in their lives. Use a suitable computer program to write up the information as a class 'Good News' paper.

Drawing Conclusions

Look at the different good news stories. Do they have anything in common? What makes a story good news?

Exploring Christian Belief

Jesus said he had come to preach the good news: the good news of God's love and forgiveness, the good news that God invites all to join his family.

Note Choose suitable local newspapers. Go through the papers beforehand and make sure the bad news they contain is suitable for the age of the children.

GOOD NEWS

FRIEND SAVES BOY DROWNING

£10,000 raised for charity

Aid reaches famine area

War ends

Assembly Ideas

Run a series of assemblies on local or national good news stories. End with Jesus' good news.

Do a simple treasure hunt in assembly and encourage the children to share their stories of the Treasure in the Field.

Ask the children to read their party menus and tell the story of the Great Feast (page 72).

WRITING

The Fish

In the early days of Christianity, it was too dangerous to admit openly that you were a follower of Jesus. Christians often ended up as food for the lions in the arena.

The early Christians used a fish as a secret sign. They drew the fish sign on the ground so that they could recognize each other.

Greek was a language used by many people at the time of Jesus. The word for FISH in Greek is ICHTHUS. In Greek letters it looks like this:

Christians chose a fish for their secret sign because each Greek letter stood for a word. Together the words made up the main Christian belief about Jesus.

Greek		English
Ι	**I**esous	Jesus
Χ	**Ch**ristos	Christ
Θ	**Th**eou	God's
Υ	**U**ios	Son
Σ	**S**oter	Saviour

This is a form of **acrostic**.

Activity

Make up your own acrostic poem. Write a word down the side of your page. The subject of your poem should be the same as this word.

Start the first line of your poem with the first letter in your word. Start the second line with the second letter, and so on.

Activity

Make up a secret acrostic which Christians today could use.

Exploring Christian Belief

Talk through the meaning of the fish acrostic and the need for secret signs. Discuss how difficult it is to stand up for what you believe to be right when people laugh at you. Talk about how difficult it must have been for early Christians who faced persecution.

Men Like Trees Walking

Activity

Read the story of Jesus healing the blind man.

When Jesus healed the blind man, the man said he saw 'men like trees walking'. That is what men looked like to him.

What else might he have seen? How do you think he would have described these things?

Start your poem with 'Men like trees walking' then add more lines. For example:

Men like trees walking
Birds like kites flying
Eyes like pools swimming

Note The children will need a copy of the story of the healing of the blind man (page 73) for this activity.

I Am

Jesus described himself using seven 'I am' sayings:

I am the bread of life.
I am the way, the truth and the life.
I am the light of the world.
I am the vine (grape-vine).
I am the door or gateway.
I am the resurrection and the life.
I am the good shepherd.

Most of these are **metaphors**. Jesus was not really a plant or baked in the oven. Jesus used lots of metaphors to help people understand who he was.

What Is a Metaphor?

A metaphor is when you describe one thing as something else. Jesus described himself as food (bread), as a plant (grape-vine) and as furniture (a door).

If you had to describe yourself as food, what food would you be? What best describes the sort of person you are?

If you had to describe yourself as a plant, what plant would you be?

If you had to describe yourself as a piece of furniture, what piece of furniture would you be?

Activity

Think of a well-known person. If you had to describe them under the headings below, what would you describe them as? The examples are characters from the Bible.

	Food	Colour	Furniture/ Building	Plant
Goliath	swede	purple	sky scraper	thistle
Mary	celery	dark red	armchair	willow tree

Think About It

What do you think Jesus meant by describing himself as a vine etc.? Look at the list of 'I am' sayings and discuss with a friend what you think they mean.

Exploring Christian Belief

Go through lots of metaphors with the children until they understand what they are. This is an activity for older children. Continually ask them why they chose particular colours etc. What do their choices say about that person's character? Let the children share what they think the 'I am' sayings mean. There are traditional interpretations of these. The children can write to local Christians asking them to explain what they understand by these sayings.

Note Developing this skill in children is important as metaphors are used widely in poetry.

Kennings

Activity

A **kenning** is an ancient Viking way of describing something or someone without actually using the name. For example:

- A caterpillar could be a 'leaf-cruncher'.
- A butterfly could be a 'sky-swimmer'.

Think up some kennings for Jesus and make them into a poem. For example:

Heart-healer
Life-giver
Word-sharpener
Storm-stopper

Assembly Ideas

Play the song 'You're the Tops', which is full of metaphors. Run a series of assemblies on the 'I Am' sayings. Use some of the children's metaphors where appropriate.

Let the children share their kennings for Jesus and explain why they chose that particular description.

Tell the story of the blind man (page 73) and read the children's poems.

Demonstrate the ICHTHUS acrostic and read some of the children's acrostic poems.

A Story Frieze: The Lost Sheep

Activity

As a group or a class, try to design a frieze of the story of the Lost Sheep that will express how lonely and frightened the lost sheep was and how safe and secure the other ninety-nine were. Try to show how difficult and dangerous it was for the shepherd to find the lost sheep.

Making Sheep

How could you make a hundred sheep as a group or class? What method could you use? Are you going to make each sheep separately or find a way of mass producing them?

Assembly Line

You might like to set up an assembly line. This is a method of mass production many factories use.

1. Decide on a method of making sheep.

Example   Make a sheep template. Cut sheep from card and print white 'wool' using a stick of Quadro or a large drinking-straw dipped in white paint.

2. Divide your method of making sheep into separate jobs.

Example   (a) Draw round the template.
(b) Cut out the sheep.
(c) Print the wool.

3. Organize people to do each job.

Example   Put three people in a row sitting at tables. The first draws a sheep on card using a template and passes it to the second person, who cuts it out. The third person prints the wool.

4. Each person should have all the items they need (scissors etc.) in front of them. You will need back-up staff to make sure all these items are there and to remove the finished sheep.

What problems do you think you will meet?

The Background

How could you make a background that looks dangerous for the shepherd in the dark? What materials could you use?

How could you make a sheep pen? Remember to place one sheep far away from the others.

Exploring Christian Belief

Talk with the children about being lost and what it feels like. Discuss what it must be like for the parents when a child is lost. In the story of the Lost Sheep (page 71) Jesus likens himself to a good shepherd who cares for each individual sheep and is prepared to risk his own life for his sheep. This was not a new idea: in Psalm 23 David likens God to a good shepherd.

ART

Symbols of Jesus

The Chi Rho

Christians call Jesus 'The Christ'. This is a title which means 'special king'.

The word for CHRIST in Greek is CHRISTOS. In Greek letters it starts like this:

This is the letter Chi:

This is the letter Rho:

The Chi Rho is just the first two letters put on top of each other.

IHS

These are three of the letters of the name Jesus in Greek. They are often put together to form a pattern.

Could you form a pattern out of the first three letters of your name?

Alpha and Omega

Alpha is the first letter of the Greek alphabet. It has the same sound as 'a' in English. A capital alpha looks like this: A

It is where the word **alpha**bet comes from.

Omega is the last letter of the Greek alphabet. It sound like the 'o' in 'note'. A capital omega looks like this: Ω

Alpha and omega is a sign for Jesus. It means beginning and end. Christians believe that Jesus was with God at the beginning of the world helping God create it. He will still be there at the end of time.

Activity

Design a badge for a Christian using one of these signs for Jesus.

Activity

How could you turn your own name into a sign? Design a badge for yourself using a design made from your name.

Exploring Christian Belief

Often secret symbols were used because it was dangerous to be a follower of Jesus. Talk with the children about standing up for what you believe in and how difficult that can be. It was more than difficult for the early Christians. It often cost them their lives.

ART

Jesus in Art

Nobody knows exactly what Jesus looked like. He was born in Palestine and probably had the dark colouring of people of that region.

Activity

Collect books containing pictures of Jesus and make a display of them. Do the pictures say anything about his character?

Choose one picture to look at more closely. How would you describe the Jesus in this picture? Kind, fierce, gentle?

Which picture do you like most of all? Give a reason for your answer.

Which picture do you like least? Why?

Exploring Christian Belief

Christianity is a world faith but each country tends to draw Jesus like themselves. In England Jesus used to be drawn with fair hair and blue eyes. Indian Christians draw Jesus as Indian and African Christians draw him as an African. This may need handling sensitively with some children, particularly Jewish and Muslim children. Do not ask them to draw pictures of Jesus.

Note An excellent pack of posters of Jesus from a variety of cultures, *Jesus Worldwide*, is available from CEM, Royal Buildings, Victoria Street, Derby DE1 1GW.

Assembly Ideas

Do three assemblies on symbols of Jesus and explain their origins. Encourage the children to show their designs.

Take three assemblies on a 'lost' theme using the stories of the Lost Sheep (page 71), the Lost Coin and the Lost Son, all of which occur in Luke 15.

ART

Songs About Jesus

These songs show how Christians from different cultures express their faith in Jesus.

Jesu Tawa Pano

This song comes from Zimbabwe. The words mean: Jesus, we are here (×3); we are here for you. Lord Jesus.

Brightly

Words and music © Patrick Matsikenyiri

Je - su ta - wa pa - no; Je - su ta - wa pa - no;

(except last time)

Je - su ta - wa pa - no; ta - wa pa - no, mu zi - ta re - nyu.

Mambo Je-su.

Puji Yesu

This song comes from India. The words mean: Thank you, thank you Jesus (×3) In my heart.

Arranged by Sue Hatherly

Pu - ji Pu - ji Ye - su __ Pu - ji Pu - ji Ye - su __ Pu - ji Pu - ji Ye-su-di-ha ti ku. _____

Pu - ji Pu - ji Ye - su __ Pu - ji Pu - ji Ye - su __ Pu - ji Pu - ji Ye-su-di-ha ti ku.

Activity

Find out how Christians from your area express their faith in Jesus in music.

Exploring Christian Belief

Explore the ideas in these songs. What Christian beliefs are they expressing about Jesus? If appropriate, children can learn to sing these songs. If that is not suitable you may be able to get a church group to sing them for you.

Note Two excellent sources of multicultural Christian songs are *Many and Great* and *Sent by the Lord*. Both are published by Wild Goose Publications and are available in tape and book form from Chansitor Publications Ltd, St Mary's Works, St Mary's Plain, Norwich NR3 3BH.

MUSIC

Music from History

Throughout history Christians have expressed their faith in Jesus through music. Here are some examples of songs about Jesus from different ages:

'O Gladsome Light' (words third century, tune sixteenth century)
'Be Thou My Vision' (early Irish tune and words)
'O Come, O Come, Immanuel' (twelfth century)
'God Be in My Head' (sixteenth century, Sarum primer)
'While Shepherds Watched', by Nahum Tate (seventeenth century)
'How Sweet the Name of Jesus Sounds', by John Newton (eighteenth century)
'What a Friend We Have in Jesus', by Joseph M. Scriven (nineteenth century)
'Lord of the Dance', by Sidney Carter (twentieth century)

Note Many of these hymns can be found in *Hymns of Faith* (Scripture Union). 'Lord of the Dance' appears in *Faith Folk and Clarity* (Galliard Press) and 'God Be in My Head' is printed on p. 106. An excellent source of simple historical music is the series *Music from the Past* (four books), published by Longman.

Activity

Look through hymn-books and see if you can create a life of Jesus in song. Start with carols about his birth and move on to his life and teaching, his death and resurrection.

Make a collage of the songs and add pictures to illustrate the life of Jesus.

Activity

Look for songs about Jesus written at different times in the past. Make a time-line of music about Jesus, pasting the songs along the line together with pictures of people of the period. If possible, invite someone to play the songs for you.

Who Am I?

This is a question-and-answer game. One person decides to be a character from a book or television. The rest of the class or group ask them questions. The person being questioned can only answer 'Yes', 'No', or 'Don't know'.

Exploring Christian Belief

Jesus asked his disciples a similar question: 'Who do people say that I am?' He was not playing a game. He wanted to know what people thought about him. Here is what his disciples replied:

'Some say you are Elijah or one of the prophets. Others say you are John the Baptist come back to life.'

'Who do you think I am, Peter?'

'You are the Christ [God's special king]'.

Christians today would answer that same question with Peter's words. They believe that Jesus is the special king that God had promised, the Christ or Messiah.

JESUS' BIRTH 100 200 300 400 500 600 700 800 900 1000 1100 1200 1300 1400 1500 1600 1700 1800 1900 2000

Lord of the dance

MUSIC

DRAMA

Jesus' Job

God has sent me to bring good news to the
poor,
To heal the broken hearted
and to comfort the sad
To set the captives free,
To give sight to the blind,
To free the oppressed.

(Isaiah 61; Luke 4)

When Jesus started his work he used a passage from Isaiah to explain his job. Some of this description of the work of Jesus can be explored through drama.

Warm-up

Play 'What's My Line', where children mime a job and the others have to guess what it is.

Preach the Good News

1. News can be met in many ways: people may welcome it, reject it, ignore it, or get angry. The children can explore these different responses in a series of sketches. Put the children in pairs and give one partner an item of good news. They must attempt to share this with the other partner. Give the other partner a piece of paper with a response on it (bored, angry, glad etc.). They have to respond to the good news in the way their piece of paper directs.

2. Sit each group in a circle. The first person says, 'The good news is . . .' and adds some good news.

> The good news is that there is no school tomorrow.

The next person responds with 'The bad news is . . .' and adds their own item of bad news related to the good news just given. Magic and nonsense are not allowed.

> The bad news is they are giving us work to do at home.

The children carry on alternating good and bad news round the circle until they get back to the person who started the game.

3. Ask the children to sit and think quietly about good news they have received. What is the best piece of news they have ever had?

Exploring Christian Belief

Jesus said he came to preach the good news. The word 'gospel' just means good news. Explore with the children what that good news was and how various people responded to it.

Set the Captive Free

Each child can imagine they are in a small cell. Ask them to feel their way all around it inch by inch to make sure there are no gaps they can escape through.

Groups of children can be prison walls with one child in the centre. The walls can close ranks as the prisoner tries to escape.

Children can try walking as if wearing chains or a ball and chain.

Talk with the children about the invisible prisons people build for themselves: prisons of fear, hate, loneliness, pride etc.

Give Sight to the Blind

Explore in drama a little of what blindness means, but make it plain to the children that this is only a tiny glimpse.

- Children can take it in turns to wear a blindfold and practise leading each other safely round the room. Obstacles can be placed around the room but these must be soft. The emphasis must be on safety.
- Set up a 'feely' table where the children can try guessing what the items are by touch.
- Provide a selection of clothes. Can the children select outfits by touch? Would they like to wear those combinations?
- Do foods taste different if you can't see them?
- Are other people still there if you can't see them or do voices come at you from nowhere?
- Can you tell what size room you are in if you close your eyes?

Discuss other types of blindness with the children. Can people be 'blind' to suffering or injustice?

Exploring Christian Belief

Discuss these various parts of Jesus' job with the children. Jesus told his followers to carry on his work: to heal the sick, comfort the distressed, and work for justice, to carry on spreading the good news. This work can be followed up by looking at people who have carried on Jesus' job, e.g. Dr Barnardo or Mother Teresa.

DRAMA

Shadow Puppets

Shadow puppets are popular in parts of Asia. These puppets are placed behind a screen with a light behind them. The shadow of the puppet then falls on the screen.

Making Shadow Puppets

Cut a flat puppet from card. Attach a garden cane to its back.

Make a screen from a clean sheet and place a light behind it.

Place your puppet behind the screen so that its shadow falls directly on it.

You can also make puppets with movable arms and legs. How could you do this?

Making Overhead-projector Puppets

You can also put puppets on an overhead projector to make shadows on a screen.

Make a simple card figure. Attach a strip of card or thick acetate to the back of the figure so that you can lift it on and off the projector.

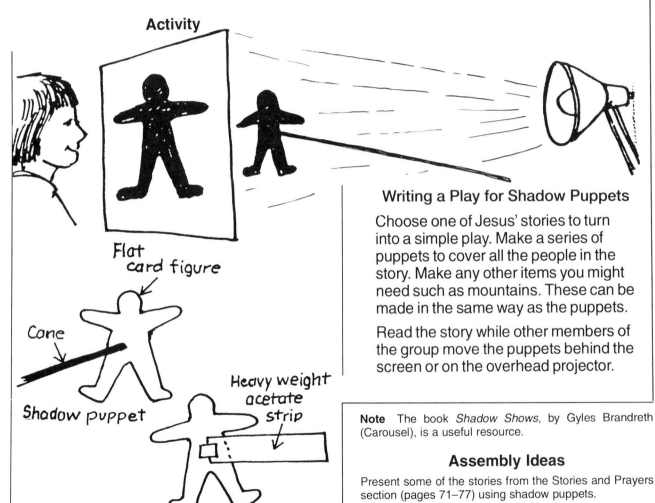

Activity

Flat card figure

Cone

Shadow puppet

Heavy weight acetate strip

OHP puppet

Writing a Play for Shadow Puppets

Choose one of Jesus' stories to turn into a simple play. Make a series of puppets to cover all the people in the story. Make any other items you might need such as mountains. These can be made in the same way as the puppets.

Read the story while other members of the group move the puppets behind the screen or on the overhead projector.

Note The book *Shadow Shows*, by Gyles Brandreth (Carousel), is a useful resource.

Assembly Ideas

Present some of the stories from the Stories and Prayers section (pages 71–77) using shadow puppets.

Run a series of assemblies on Jesus' job, exploring a different part each day. Encourage the children to participate in various dramatic interpretations.

Leaders

Warm-up

The children can play games such as 'Follow the Leader', where one person leads a long line around the hall. Children can also play games such as 'Simon Says', where the rest of the class have to follow the leader's instructions.

Activity

Invent an imaginary leader of the class. Think about the qualities leaders need (what sort of people they need to be) and the difficulties of the job.

Draw round someone in the class. Inside the figure write the qualities that the imaginary class leader would need.

Round the outside of the figure write the help a leader would need from the rest of the class. Leaders cannot act alone.

Activity

Look at Jesus' qualities as a leader.

Draw round someone in the class. Add first-century clothes to the figure.

Round the outside write Jesus' qualities as a leader.

Activity

Leaders need followers. What makes a good follower or disciple?

Draw round someone in the class. This time write the qualities of a follower inside the figure.

Exploring Christian Belief

Children can discuss the ways we get our leaders and the various ways leaders come to power. This might be a time for looking at good and bad leaders. Christians regard Jesus as their leader. They did not elect him. They believe he is a leader because they believe he is God's son. Many people follow Jesus because they believe he is wise, caring and strong. He showed he could be a strong leader. Jesus never promised his followers an easy life. He did not persuade people to follow him, in fact he often told people to go away and think it over because it was a very important step to take. Jesus requires certain things of his followers like love, loyalty and service.

Names for Jesus

Hello, my name is Lidia. I am a Christian from Tanzania. As Christians we call Jesus 'Saviour'. In our language we use the word 'Mwokozi'.

A Mwokozi is a person who rescues you from a dangerous situation. Imagine you are about to be attacked by a wild animal such as a cheetah or a lion and you have no way of defending yourself. You are carrying no weapons. The person who rescues you from this danger is called your Mwokozi.

Jesus is our Mwokozi, the one who rescues us from the dangers of wrong, the one who loves and protects us. At night we pray: 'Our Mwokozi, keep us alive this night till morning.'

My name is Shamem. I am a Christian from Pakistan. We call Jesus 'Badsha' or 'King' because we accept him as our king. At Easter we often call him 'Masih-e-maslub', which means 'Christ Crucified', and we remember that Jesus died for us. Jesus is also known as 'Yesu-yar', which means 'Jesus the friend', the friend who never lets us down.

My name is Fazal. I'm also a Christian from Pakistan. We add the name Masih to our names to show that we are followers of Jesus. The word 'Masih' means Messiah or Christ (special king).

Activity

Visit a local church and see if you can find different titles for Jesus around the building, in the hymn-books, in the service books or on banners.

Alternatively, interview some Christians about the different titles used for Jesus and why they are used.

PAST/PRESENT

Cross-curricular Links

The background to Jesus' life provides many opportunities for cross-curricular work.

History

The historical background will help the children understand the world into which Jesus was born: the expanding Roman Empire. It will also help them understand Jesus' teaching. Israel was an occupied country. The enemy was on the streets and armed. This was the enemy Jesus asked people to love.

Citizenship

Family life, education and the world of work in first-century Israel can be explored.

Technology

The children can look at how houses in Israel were designed in the time of Jesus. They can then investigate the conditions which caused them to be designed in that way. Middle Eastern houses can be made by the children. The houses can be put together to form a street and incidents/stories from the life of Jesus added to form a frieze. This is the idea central to the video *Luke Street* (Scripture Union), which contains eight short stories centred on houses which occur in the gospel of Luke (4:38–40; 5:18–25; 7:36–39, 44–47; 8:40–42, 49–56; 10:38–42; 19:1–8; 22:14–22; 24:28–35).

Geography

On a map of the Middle East, places which featured in Jesus' life (Bethlehem, Egypt, Jerusalem, Nazareth, Cana etc.) can be marked. The names can be related to their modern counterparts.

The geography of the area can be explored: its physical features, climate etc. How did clothes worn at the time of Jesus reflect the climate?

With older children, data on rainfall and temperature can be compared with the climate they experience.

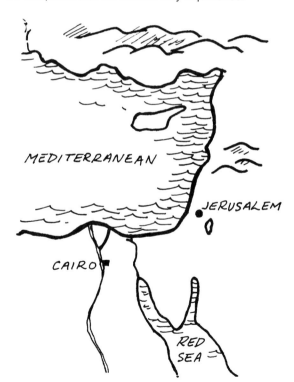

Fiction

The Narnia Books, by C. S. Lewis (Puffin).
The Finnglas Series, by Fay Sampson (Lion). These are books for top juniors. The Jesus figure in these is a dolphin.

Other Useful Books

Life in the Time of Jesus, by M. Keene (Oliver and Boyd).
Life in Bible Times, by C. Tarrant (Scripture Union).
Jesus, Who Are You? by S. Phillips (Longman).
Jesus and the Kingdom, by S. Phillips (Longman).
Jesus the Trouble Maker, by S. Phillips (Longman).
Learning about Jesus, by F. Henderson (Lion).
Jesus, Centre of Controversy – Do It Yourself Cartoons, by R. Castle (Bible Society). Contains tape and duplicating masters.
Jesus, Man of Action – Do It Yourself Cartoons, by R. Castle (Bible Society). Contains tape and duplicating masters.

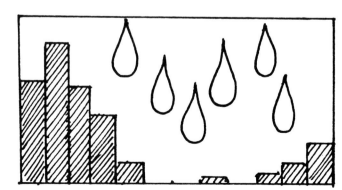

A Christian Puzzle

Activity

Look at the word square below. It is a Roman puzzle square. It has been found scratched on walls as far apart as Cirencester and Pompeii.

The square was probably written by Christians. It is in code. Can you crack the code? Look at the square closely. What do you notice about it?

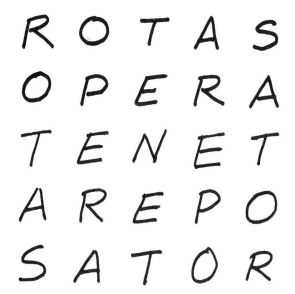

R O T A S
O P E R A
T E N E T
A R E P O
S A T O R

Clue 1 The square is written in Latin. The words mean 'Arepo the sower holds the wheel tightly'.

Clue 2 Look at the shape the word TENET makes.

Clue 3 Look up Mark 4:1–20 in the Bible to find out who the sower might be.

Clue 4 Copy the letters of the puzzle square onto squared paper and then cut them up. If you rearrange the letters in the shape drawn below, you can make the words PATER NOSTER twice with an extra O and A.

```
        A
        P
        A
        T
        E
        R
A PATERNOSTER O
        O
        S
        T
        E
        R
        O
```

Clue 5 The words 'Pater Noster' mean 'Our Father'. Do you know a prayer that starts 'Our Father'?

Clue 6 Many Romans also knew some Greek. The letters A (alpha) and O (omega) are the first and last letters of the Greek alphabet. Read Revelation 22:13 in the Bible. Jesus called himself 'Alpha and Omega'. Why do you think Christians who used this puzzle square included alpha and omega?

Activity

Make up your own puzzle square with a hidden message in it.

Exploring Christian Belief

Mark 4 contains the parable of the Sower, in which Jesus himself is the sower who sows the word of God. You will find the Lord's Prayer in the topic 'Prayer and Worship' (page 97). 'Alpha and Omega' is a title for Jesus meaning he is the beginning and the end. This puzzle is probably a Christian secret code, written because followers of Jesus were persecuted. In dangerous times it may have reminded them that Jesus could hold them fast (*tenet*).

Assembly Ideas

Crack a large version of the code in assembly. Talk about people who are suffering for their beliefs today and/or those who suffered in the past. You might like to talk about the work of Amnesty International.

Gingerbread Men

Gingerbread used to be eaten at celebration meals. Through the winter months, when fresh food was not available, the spicy flavour of ginger made a welcome change.

Sometimes gingerbread was made in the shape of a man, representing Jesus. These gingerbread men were sometimes given as presents. Many of them were decorated so that they made an extra special present.

At first gingerbread was made of sweetened, flavoured crumbs pressed in moulds and then baked so that it was like a biscuit. Later moist sticky gingerbread was popular. Modern gingerbread men are more like a biscuit. This is a modern recipe but an old custom.

Activity

Make some packaging for a gingerbread man that will protect it and stop it breaking. Your packaging should also be safe, attractive and allow the shopper to see the gingerbread man.

Recipe for Gingerbread Men

You will need

45 g soft brown sugar
85 g golden syrup
1 level teaspoon ground ginger
½ level teaspoon ground cinnamon
good pinch of nutmeg
50 g margarine
235 g plain flour
1 level teaspoon bicarbonate of soda
½ beaten egg
currants and glacé cherries

small bowl or cup
saucepan
wooden spoon
rolling-pin
man-shaped cutter
baking-tray
wire rack

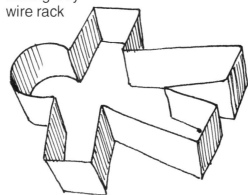

Method

Ask an adult to set the oven to gas mark 3/170°C (325°F).

1. Put the sugar, syrup and spices in a saucepan and heat slowly until almost boiling.

2. Remove from the heat.

3. Cut the margarine into small pieces and add to the hot sugar mixture. Stir until it has melted.

4. Beat in the flour, bicarbonate of soda and egg.

5. Knead on a floured board until smooth.

6. Roll out to the thickness of a 10p piece.

7. Cut out men with a cutter.

8. Place the men on a baking-tray.

9. Bake for 10–15 minutes.

10. When cooked leave to cool on a wire rack.

11. Decorate with currants for eyes and slices of cherry for a mouth.

COOKING

		Page	English	Maths	Science	Technology
Stories and Prayers	Stories Jesus Told about Prayer	96	1, 2, 3			
	The Lord's Prayer	97	2, 3			5
	Praise Prayers	97	1, 3			
	Thank-you Prayers	98	2, 3			
	Sorry Prayers	98	1, 2, 3			1, 2, 3, 4
	Praying for Yourself and Others	99	2, 3			
	Help Prayers: An SOS to God	99	1, 2			
	Aids to Prayer	100	1			
	Graces	101	1, 3			
	Amy Carmichael: Does God Answer Prayer?	101	1		4	1, 2, 3, 4
	Worship	102	2, 3			
	The Heart of Worship	103	1			
Writing	The Friend at Midnight	104	2, 3			
	Calligrams	104	3			
	The Pharisee and the Tax-collector	104	2, 3			
	Letters to God	104	1, 2, 3			
	Fan Clubs	105	1, 2, 3			
	Word Collections	105	1, 2, 3, 4			
Poetry	Prayer Poems	106	1, 2, 3			
	Couplets and Triplets	107	1, 2, 3			
	Animal Prayers	107	2, 3			
Art	Praying Hands	108	1, 2			
	Through the Window	109	1			
	Banners and Kneelers	110	1, 2, 3			
	Christian Buildings	110	1	4		
Music	Yesuve Saranam	111	1, 2			
	It's Me, O Lord	112	1, 2			
	Let Us Break Bread Together	113	1, 2			
	Music for Worship	114	1, 2, 3			
Drama	Dance in Worship	115	1, 2			
	Offering Presents	116	1			
PSE	Communication	117	1, 2, 3			
Past/Present	How Some Christians Pray	118	1			
Cross-curricular links	Technology	118	1	1, 2, 4		1, 2, 3, 4
	Maths	118	1	1, 4, 5		5
	Christianity: A World Faith	118	1			
	History	119	1, 2, 3			
Games	The Hand Game	119	1, 3			
Cooking	Pretzels	120	1, 2	2	3	

NATIONAL CURRICULUM KEY

Attainment Targets	English
1	Speaking and listening
2	Reading
3	Writing
4	Spelling
5	Handwriting
4/5	Presentation

	Maths
1	Using and applying maths
2	Number
3	Algebra
4	Shape and space
5	Handling data

	Science
1	Scientific investigation
2	Life and living processes
3	Materials and their properties
4	Physical processes

	Technology
1	Identifying needs and opportunities
2	Generating a design
3	Planning and making
4	Evaluating
5	Information Technology capability

PRAYER AND WORSHIP

UNDERSTANDING
CHRISTIAN CONCEPTS ABOUT
PRAYER AND WORSHIP

Prayer and worship are not separate entities, there is a degree of overlap. Prayer is part of worship but worship is far more than prayer. Prayer is communication with God, worship is adoration of God.

Prayer

1. Christians believe they should pray because communicating with God is part of their friendship with him. They also believe God listens and wants to answer prayer. A prayer answered 'No' or 'Wait' is not an unanswered prayer: the answer is merely different to what the person wanted. An answer may come through an inner feeling or certainty, it may come through the words of the Bible or it may come through other people.

2. Jesus taught that prayer is not a bargain or an attempt to make God do what people want. God is on humanity's side before people pray. Prayer is God allowing human beings to share in the running of the world. It is a way of life for a Christian not just an event that happens at certain times.

3. Prayer can be completely silent or spoken out loud or in one's head. There are many types of prayer:

   - *Praise*   This is telling God how great he is.
   - *Thanks*   This is thanking God for what he has done.
   - *Confession*   This is saying sorry for wrong-doing, asking for forgiveness and help to change.

   - *Asking*   Asking prayers can be for oneself or others. These are not a slot-machine type of prayer or a letter to Santa. They are always said with the provision that what is asked for must be within God's will. Christians expect God to say 'No' to things that would be harmful or wrong.
   - *Help*   These are SOS-type prayers often said in times of stress or trouble.
   - *Just chatting*   Prayers do not have to be said in any particular language or voice or in any particular place. Many 'prayers' are just chatting to God as you would to a parent or friend.
   - *Silent prayer*   Prayer is often wordless. It is just enjoying being with someone, knowing they know your needs etc. It is like sitting near a very good friend, or with a parent, when there is no need for words.

4. Christians pray in various ways. Some use a set form of words. Some use icons or rosary beads to help them. Others pray silently. There is no one type of prayer.

Worship

1. Adoration is central to Christian worship. The Israelites were told to worship God with all their heart (will and emotions), with all their strength (body) and with all their mind (reason). The body is used in Christian worship in dance, drama and ritual, the mind is used in thinking about God's message and the emotions are used when people respond to God with their feelings.

2. People can worship in many ways: in song, prayer, drama, ritual, liturgy (a set pattern of words) and dance, through art and architecture, through poetry and story. All these can be elements of worship.

3. Christians believe their life ought to be an act of worship: a gift to God, a way of saying 'Thank you'.

4. For many Christians the heart of worship is Mass or Communion (also called Breaking of Bread or the Eucharist or the Lord's Supper). This is a time when Jesus' death is remembered and his presence especially felt.

5. School worship may be the only experience that some children have of worship. It must be emphasized that collective worship in schools is different from the corporate worship of a body of believers. In some schools, however, a positive experience of school collective worship will help a child understand the worship of a believing community.

This subject of prayer and worship is extremely wide. Some of the material on prayer and worship is in the Stories and Prayers section. Some of it has been put under subject headings such as Drama, Art etc. because this is where it can be explored most naturally.

Stories Jesus Told about Prayer

The Pharisee and the Tax-collector

Two men went into the Temple to pray. One was a Pharisee, a religious leader, respected by all the people. The other was a tax-collector, hated and despised by everyone.

The religious leader stood up before God feeling very proud of himself and said, 'I thank you, God, that I am not like other people, not like that horrible tax-collector over there.'

The tax-collector, on the other hand, was so sorry for the wrong he had done that he hung his head and asked God to forgive him. Jesus said it was the tax-collector's prayer that God was pleased with.

(*Luke 18:9–14*)

The Friend at Midnight

Late one night a man was woken up by a loud knocking on his door. Crossly the man shouted, 'Who is it?'

'It's only me,' answered his neighbour. 'A friend of mine has just arrived and I have no food to give him. Can you lend me three loaves?'

'No I can't!' said the man grumpily. 'The whole family are asleep and I am not getting up just for that.'

The neighbour did not give up. He kept knocking at the door until the man gave in and fetched him the bread for the sake of peace and quiet. (*Luke 11:5–8*)

The Woman Who Would Not Give Up

In a certain town lived a judge who was hard and unfeeling. In the same town lived a poor widow who kept coming to him and saying,

'Can you please see that I am treated fairly?'

The judge refused to do anything about the poor widow's case but the widow kept pestering him. After a while he said to himself, 'Although I don't care about this woman's situation she is pestering me to death! I'll sort out her case so that she stops coming and annoying me with her constant nagging.' (*Luke 18:1–8*)

Stones, Snakes and Scorpions

If your children ask you for bread would you give them stones instead? If they ask for a fish would you give them snakes? If they ask for eggs no loving parent would give them scorpions.

If you know how to give good gifts to your children, how much more does God!

(*Luke 11:11–12; Matthew 7:9–11*)

Activity

Rewrite the story of Stones, Snakes and Scorpions, but invent your own three unpleasant gifts. Use gifts that will help children today understand the meaning of the story. For example:

If your children asked for fish you would not give them a slug.

What gifts might a child ask for that a parent would not give?

Exploring Christian Belief

Jesus wanted to make people realize how eager God is to listen to prayer. Jesus said God is *not* like either the judge or the friend: he does not answer prayer because he has been nagged into doing it, he wants to answer prayer just as parents want to give good things to their children. Christians believe God hears prayer but he will not give people anything harmful or wrong for them.

Note More activities on these stories can be found in the Writing section (page 104).

STORIES AND PRAYERS

The Lord's Prayer

One day Jesus' disciples asked him to teach them how to pray. He taught them this prayer:

Our Father in heaven:
May your holy name be honoured;
May your kingdom come;
May your will be done on earth as it is in heaven.
Give us today the food we need.
Forgive us the wrongs we have done,
As we forgive the wrongs that others have done to us.
Do not bring us to the hard testing,
But keep us safe from the Evil One.

(*Matthew 6:9–13*)

Activity

Type this prayer on the word processor leaving a triple space between the lines. In the gap below each line, write what you think that line means.

Exploring Christian Belief

When his disciples asked him how they should pray, Jesus gave this prayer as an example. It is a prayer used frequently by many Christians. Jesus told his disciples to call God 'Father', which is both a familiar term and carries the idea of authority. When children have learnt to identify the different types of prayer (pages 97–99), they might like to try and find them within this prayer.

Praise Prayers

Beyond Words

I can't find the words to say it,
I can't find the songs to sing it,
I can't find the rhymes to write it
So I shall just have to feel it inside.
For I know
That you know
That I think you're great, God!

I will trust in you, God,
I will sing praises to you.
Wake up my soul! Wake up harp!
Wake up stringed instruments!
I will wake up the sun with my song.
I will tell all the nations of the earth how great you are.

(*Adapted from Psalm 108*)

Think About It

Praise is saying good things about someone. Praising God is like giving God a good report on the sort of person he is.

Activity

If you could write your own report, what good things would you want to say about yourself? Write your ideal report.

Exploring Christian Belief

A praise prayer tells God how great people think he is. Praise prayers, like all prayers, do not have to be said in church or at night. Christians believe they can pray in any place at any time and God will listen and act. They believe he is never too busy to listen to anybody.

STORIES AND PRAYERS

Thank-you Prayers

Give thanks to God for he is good,
His love lasts for ever.
Give thanks to the God of Gods,
His love lasts for ever.
Give thanks to the Lord of Lords,
His love lasts for ever.
He does great wonders in the earth,
His love lasts for ever.
He designed the universe by his
  understanding,
His love lasts for ever.
He created the earth with his wisdom,
His love lasts for ever.
He made the sun to rule the day,
His love lasts for ever,
He made the moon to rule the night.
                    (*Adapted from Psalm 136*)

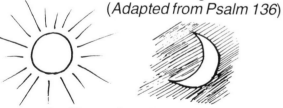

An Everyday Thank You

For nights warm beneath my duvet, when
  outside all is cold,
Thank you God.
For days playing with my friends,
Thank you God.
For food and care and all your goodness to
  me,
Thank you God.

Activity

If you look at the two thank-you prayers
you will see that they have a repeating
line. This is called a **refrain**.

Write your own thank-you prayer with a
repeating line.

Activity

Make a thank-you display from
thank-you cards, thank-you paper and
so on.

Exploring Christian Belief

Discuss being thankful and how we show it. Sometimes
we are not thankful for things until we no longer have
them. Often we are not thankful for health until we lose it.
Some people focus on what they have not got rather than
being thankful for what they have got. They moan about
what happens rather than being thankful for the things that
have not happened. Declare a 'Thank-you day' when the
children try to concentrate on the many things they have
to be thankful for. Being thankful is an attitude that can
bring joy.

Sorry Prayers

I know I have done wrong, God,
Forgive me.
I know when I hurt others, I hurt you.
You were right to correct me.
Wash me clean of all wrong and I shall be
  whiter than snow.
Rub out my wrong and make me joyful
  again.
Give me a new heart that wants to do what
  is right.   (*Adapted from Psalm 51*)

Think About It

Has there ever been a time when you have
felt sorry for something you have done and
wished you could rub it out and start again?

Activity

Design a 'sorry card' which someone
could use to write an apology.

Exploring Christian Belief

Saying sorry is how we repair a damaged relationship. It
recognizes the wrong done and is the first step towards
putting it right. For a Christian all wrong is wrong against
God because he is the creator of all. To hurt one of his
people or part of creation is to hurt him. Christians believe
everybody does things wrong, no one is perfect. They also
believe that God is willing to forgive people who are sorry
for what they have done wrong.

Praying for Yourself and Others

Solomon's Prayer

When there is a famine or disease,
When the crops fail because they have
    been eaten by locusts or burnt by
    scorching winds,
Hear our heartfelt prayer.

(Adapted from 1 Kings 8:37–38)

The Cardboard Box

There are a million things I could ask God for
So much I want
But today I saw a teenager sleeping in a
    cardboard box.
She looked like my elder sister;
She looked so cold,
So hungry,
So alone.
Suddenly I felt I had too much already, so
    my prayers are for her.
For work and food
For a home with warmth and love.

Activity

Look at a recent newspaper.
Sometimes Christians pray as they
read the newspaper. When they see
events and people that need a prayer,
they stop reading and pray for that
particular situation.

Cut out newspaper stories you think a
Christian might pray about. If you wish
you can write a prayer underneath.

Exploring Christian Belief

Discuss with the children the sorts of things they think
Christians pray for. Are there some things it would be
wrong to pray for? Prayer is not an attempt to make God
do what people want. It is taking part in a relationship. It is
being allowed to share in God's work. There are some
things which Christians should not ask for: things that
would be harmful, selfish or evil. No loving God would say
'Yes' to such requests. Children might remember parents
saying 'No' to certain things when they were young which
they now know to be dangerous.

Note Check all newspapers for unsuitable stories.

Help Prayers: An SOS to God

Rescue me, God
I'm in trouble up to my neck!
I feel as if I'm sinking in deep mud of despair,
and there is no solid ground to stand upon.
I am out of my depth,
The waves of sorrow break over me,
I'm drowning, Lord, in a sea of troubles.
Save me.

(Adapted from Psalm 69)

Activity

Find out what SOS means and how this
message is sent. What is a Mayday
call?

Exploring Christian Belief

Discuss with the children times when we need help.
Asking for help is a normal part of life. It is also a normal
part of prayer. Christians ask God for help when they are
in trouble but they try to remember to thank him when the
trouble is past.

STORIES AND PRAYERS

Aids to Prayer

The Jesus Prayer

Lord Jesus Christ
Son of God
Have mercy on me,
a sinner.

This prayer is sometimes said to the rhythm of breathing so that prayer becomes as natural as breathing in and out.

The Rosary

Some Christians use a **rosary** to help them pray. The beads are divided into different groups and each group represents a certain prayer or thought.

Activity

Find out what the different beads in a rosary stand for. Ask a Roman Catholic Christian to explain the different prayers and how a rosary helps in prayer.

Candles and Incense

Sometimes Christians light a candle or burn incense. The light and the smoke drifting upwards remind them of prayers going up to God.

They may light a candle for a person who needs help. As the candle burns they pray and think about that person.

Meditation on the Bible

Some Christians use a small section of the Bible to **meditate** on (think deeply about). They often use the words of Jesus for this. For example:

Come to me all you who are weary and burdened with care and I will give you rest.

Using Nature

Some people like to look at a natural object: a leaf, a rock, a plant or a feather, for example. They look at it closely and spend time thinking about it.

Christians believe that God made the world. Looking at something God made helps them to think about God himself.

How Christians Pray

People pray in many different ways.

Some find shutting their eyes helps them concentrate. Others like to pray with their eyes open.

Some like to keep their hands still by putting them together. Others lift their hands in prayer.

Some people like to use prayers someone else has written. Others like to make up their own prayers as they talk to God.

Think About It

If you pray, think about what helps you. What makes it harder to pray?

Activity

Interview a number of Christians from different traditions and ask them what helps them to pray.

Exploring Christian Belief

Christians believe that in prayer it is the relationship with God that matters most. How people pray and the words they use are secondary. Christians use whatever words and actions help their friendship with God. If appropriate to your school, children might like to place some candles in damp sand and use them to pray for specific people. The candles should be lit by an adult.

Graces

The word **grace** is often used to mean a prayer that is said before or after a meal. Here are a few graces:

Give me a good digestion, Lord,
And also something to digest;
But when and how that something comes
I leave to thee, who knowest best.
> (*Part of a refectory grace,
> Chester Cathedral*)

Dear Lord, bless this food for our use, and
    us for your service.   (*Celtic grace*)

God is great,
God is good,
Let us thank him for this food.

Activity

Try writing your own grace. Mount it in the centre of a paper plate.

Collect everyone's paper plates together and turn them into a display.

Exploring Christian Belief

Saying grace is one way a Christian acknowledges that ultimately all things come from God even if they were bought at the supermarket.

Amy Carmichael: Does God Answer Prayer?

When Amy Carmichael was very young she longed for blue eyes like her mother's. So she asked God to give her blue eyes. When she looked in the mirror the next day, her eyes were still a deep, dark brown. Although she was disappointed Amy did not think God had failed to answer her prayer. God had simply answered 'No'.

When Amy grew up she worked with children in India. Amy always wore Indian dress, and her dark hair and eyes helped the children to feel at home with her.

Amy spent her life caring for children in India, and the community she founded at Dohnavar still looks after children today. Amy, and many children, had good reason to be glad that God had answered 'No' to her prayer for blue eyes.

Activity

Christian children sometimes use traffic lights to show the three different answers to prayer: 'YES', 'NO' and 'WAIT'. Draw a set of traffic lights. Which answer would you put next to each colour?

If you wish you can design a set of traffic lights that light up.

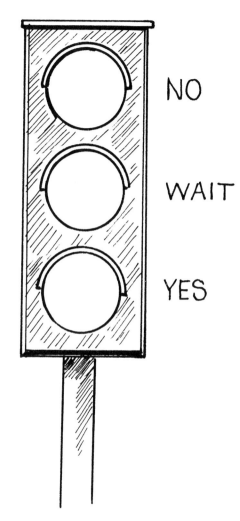

NO

WAIT

YES

Exploring Christian Belief

Although prayer is vital for a Christian, it is not easy. Christians often find it hard to understand when God does not appear to answer, and it is difficult to trust God when the answer is 'No'

Worship

Imagine being a member of a fan club and having the chance to meet, and talk to, the person you admire. What would you say to them?

Worship is about being a 'fan' of God. It is when people tell God how much they admire him. It is also offering God a gift of love and service.

Christians might sing about their love for God, read about it, act it out in drama, dance it, speak it or just silently worship God inside.

A Christian's life should be an act of worship. Every part of life should be like a present given to God.

Look at the hymn 'Take My Life'. This is a song about a person giving their whole life to God.

Take My Life

1. Take my life, and let it be
Consecrated, Lord, to Thee.
Take my moments and my days;
Let them flow in ceaseless praise.

2. Take my hands, and let them move
At the impulse of Thy love.
Take my feet, and let them be
Swift and beautiful for Thee.

3. Take my voice, and let me sing
Always, only, for my King.
Take my lips, and let them be
Filled with messages from Thee.

4. Take my silver and my gold;
Not a mite would I withhold.
Take my intellect, and use
Every power as Thou shalt choose.

5. Take my will, and make it Thine;
It shall be no longer mine.
Take my heart, it is Thine own;
It shall be Thy royal throne.

6. Take my love; my Lord, I pour
At Thy feet its treasure-store.
Take myself, and I will be
Ever, only, all for Thee.

(*Frances R. Havergal*)

Activity

Read through the hymn and list all the different parts of a Christian's life they could give to God.

Exploring Christian Belief

Worship is very important to a Christian. It should involve every part of them: their imagination, emotions, mind and body. Life itself should be lived as an act of worship: everything a Christian does should say, 'I love God.' You might like to start exploring worship by looking at the way a fan's life is influenced by the person they admire.

STORIES AND PRAYERS

The Heart of Worship

For many Christians the most important part of worship is when they meet to share bread and wine, to remember that Jesus died for them. Christians call this by different names: Mass, Communion, Eucharist, Breaking of Bread or the Lord's Supper. Christians may celebrate Communion in different ways, but for all of them it is not remembering a dead friend, but the joyous celebration of a living and present one.

The Last Supper

Before Jesus died he ate one last special meal with his friends. Jesus took the bread and broke it saying, 'This is my body broken for you.' He then took the wine, thanked God and said, 'This is my blood poured out for many. Do this to remember me.'

Every time a Christian takes part in Communion (or Mass, Breaking of Bread etc.), they are obeying Jesus' instructions to remember him in this way.

Activity

Jesus took ordinary things, bread and wine, part of the basic diet of his day, and made them special by the meaning he gave them. One of the symbols of Communion is grapes and wheat, the plants from which bread and wine are made. This symbol can be printed using fingerprints.

Dip your thumb in purple paint to print a bunch of grapes. Add the leaves and tendrils later using a paint-brush.

Dip your little finger in corn-coloured paint and use it to print a stalk of wheat. Draw the lines on later with a very thin brush or felt-tip pen.

Exploring Christian Belief

Christians may celebrate Communion in different ways but to all it is a reminder that Jesus loved people enough to die for them. This special meal is more than a reminder of Jesus' death: it is the celebration of a present and living friend by the Christian family. When telling this story to younger children emphasize the special-meal aspect. Young children find it difficult to understand the bread/body and wine/blood symbolism. The story of the Last Supper is included in more detail in the Easter topic 'Contrasts' (page 42).

Note Use paint safe for children to dip their fingers in. For more activities on worship, see the Art, Music, Drama and Poetry sections.

Assembly Ideas

Run a series on prayer exploring a different type of prayer each day. Make sure each assembly is earthed in the children's experience. For example, ask them when they get praised and read out some praise children have had written on their work.

Tell several of Jesus's stories about prayer (page 96). Children can dramatize these.

Make a large set of traffic lights and tell the story of Amy Carmichael (page 101).

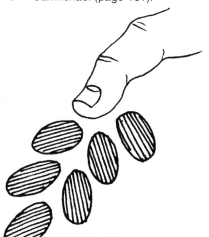

STORIES AND PRAYERS

The Friend at Midnight

Activity

Read the story of the Friend at Midnight. Imagine you are the parent in this story. You are in bed asleep and so are all your children. Suddenly there is a hammering on the door.

Tell your story using a series of cartoon boxes and captions.

Exploring Christian Belief

Jesus told this story to explain what God is not like. The story of the Woman Who Would Not Give Up (page 96) is very similar.

Note The children will need a copy of the story of the Friend at Midnight (page 96) for this activity.

Calligrams

A **calligram** is a way of making a word look like its meaning:

Activity

How could you express the following words used in prayer as calligrams?

- Thank you • great • sorry • please
  • help

The Pharisee and the Tax-collector

Activity

Read the story of the Pharisee and the Tax-collector. How could you rewrite this story with more modern characters? For example:

The Vicar and the Football Hooligan

Exploring Christian Belief

Christians believe that God listens to prayers if they are sincerely meant. That is why he was pleased with the tax-collector. The Pharisee was not really praying, he was trying to impress.

Note The children will need a copy of the story of the Pharisee and the Tax-collector (page 96) for this activity.

Letters to God

Read the children some of the *Children's Letters to God*, by E. Marshall and S. Hample (Collins/Fount). Explain that prayers can be written as well as spoken or thought. Some children might like to write their own letters to God.

WRITING

Fan Clubs

Activity

Many people admire famous people. They may be fans of a pop star, a dancer, a footballer or some other sports personality or team.

If people are fans what sorts of things do they do? What do they say about the personalities they admire?

Make a display of fan magazines, football scarves, pictures and so on.

Activity

Choose a word that describes your favourite person, group or team. Write that word in large letters on a sheet of coloured paper.

How can you decorate your word to express the feeling behind it? For example, what could you do to the word BRILLIANT to make it look brilliant?

Activity

Look at banners in a local church to see how words have been 'written' using fabric. Have Christians tried to express the meaning of the words in the way they have designed them?

Exploring Christian Belief

Talk with the children about the ways in which fans (non-violently) express their admiration. Some fans say they 'worship' their favourite personality/team. Christians worship God. They think he is great. In worship they tell God how wonderful they think he is. They might sing it, say it, act it, dance it or just quietly think it knowing that God knows what they feel. Play 'Worthy is the Lamb', the final chorus of Handel's 'Messiah'. Here Handel put to music words from the Bible praising God. For more examples see the Music section (page 114).

Word Collections

Word collections can be made for writing different types of prayer.

Create a series of pockets and ask the children what words they would put in each for that type of prayer.

Assembly Ideas

Some children might like to turn their story of the Friend at Midnight into a sketch.

Use giant calligrams to introduce the different types of prayer (pages 97–99).

Encourage the children to talk about the personalities/teams of whom they are fans. Bring in fan-club items and talk about worship of God.

WRITING

Prayer Poems

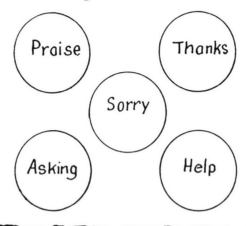

Activity

Many traditional prayers are poems. Try writing a prayer as a poem. It can be any type of prayer: thanks, saying sorry, praise, asking or calling for help.

God be in my head
and in my understanding;
God be in my eyes
and in my looking;
God be in my mouth
and in my speaking;
God be in my heart
and in my thinking;
God be at my end
and at my departing.

Let us with a gladsome mind
Praise the Lord for he is kind;
For his mercies shall endure,
Ever faithful, ever sure.

(*John Milton*)

May the road rise to meet you.
May the wind be always at your back.
May the sun shine warm upon your face,
the rains fall soft upon your fields and,
until we meet again,
may God hold you in the palm of his hand.

(*Irish blessing*)

Christ be near at either hand,
Christ above, below me stand
Christ with me wherever I go
Christ above, behind, below.

(*St Patrick*)

Activity

Make five circles on a large display area. Write in each circle the name of a different type of prayer.

Look through various prayer-books and make a copy of prayers you like. Blu-Tak each prayer in the circle you think it belongs in. Try to find at least one prayer for each circle.

What are you going to do if a prayer fits in more than one circle? For example, a prayer might contain both thanks and asking.

Exploring Christian Belief

Discuss the way we talk to friends and family. Christians believe prayer is the communication that makes a friendship with God work. It is like telephoning a friend or parent when we are away from home. It is keeping in touch. We do not restrict our conversation to asking for things, similarly prayer is more than asking. (The different types of prayer are explained on page 95.) Often children say, 'Why bother to pray if God knows everything anyway?' Christians pray for the reasons they would talk to a friend or a parent.

Note Check your photocopying licence when copying items from prayer-books.

Couplets and Triplets

Couplets

A **couplet** is a two-lined poem that rhymes. Each line has the same number of beats or syllables.

Triplets

A **triplet** is a three-lined poem that rhymes. Each line has the same number of beats or syllables.

Rhymes

Words that **rhyme** have the same sound. For example:

- 'hat' and 'cat' • 'ring' and 'sing'
- 'gold' and 'old' • 'fat' and 'mat'

Think up some more words which rhyme.

Half-rhymes

If you find it difficult to find a rhyme you can use a **half-rhyme**. A half-rhyme is when words share a similar sound. For example:

- 'home' and 'phone' • 'limp' and 'lump'
- 'flame' and 'rain'

Think up some more half-rhymes.

Activity

As a class or group, write a thank-you prayer as a couplet or a triplet. Here are some couplets:

Thank you for:

Chocolate ice cream (5)
And my football team (5)

Strawberry jelly (5)
And colour telly (5)

A day off school (4)
The swimming-pool (4)

To write a triplet, you would add one more line which rhymed with the other two and also had the same number of beats.

Exploring Christian Belief

Christians believe they can pray about anything as long as it is not wrong. For example, you should not ask God to give you all the answers in a maths test: that would be cheating. It would not be right to ask God to give all the opposing football team tummy ache, or to give you millions of pounds. Prayers do not have to be about 'religious' matters. Christians believe God cares about all the everyday things in life.

Note   With younger children this is best done as a class activity.

Animal Prayers

Prayer of the Ox

Dear God, give me time,
Men are always so driven!
Make them understand that I can never hurry.
Give me time to eat.
Give me time to plod.
Give me time to sleep.
Give me time to think.
Amen.

(Translated by Rumer Godden)

Prayer of the Little Ducks

Dear God,
give us a flood of water.
Let it rain tomorrow and always.
Give us plenty of little slugs
and other luscious things to eat.
Protect all folk who quack
and everyone who knows how to swim.
Amen.

(Translated by Rumer Godden)

POETRY

Activity

Make up your own prayer by an animal. Write it inside an animal shape.

Think About It

These animals 'pray' about things they need and like. What do you think Christians pray for?

Exploring Christian Belief

Christians do not just pray for everything they want, neither do they pray for an easy life. Their prayer has a particular pattern. First of all they tell God how they feel about him, how good he is (praise), then they thank him for all he has done and they say sorry for what they have done wrong (confession). They next ask God to help certain people and only then they pray for their own needs. This is always balanced by accepting that God may answer 'No', God may have other ideas.

Assembly Ideas

Run a series of assemblies on animal prayers. Talk about each animal and how the prayer reflects that animal's needs. Finish with a human prayer and how prayer reflects our needs.

Run a series on famous prayers. Tell the children a little about the author and the background to the prayer. For helpful books see page 119.

Praying Hands

Albrecht Dürer was a great German artist. He came from a large, but not very well off family. Albrecht's friend, who was also an artist, worked to earn enough money for both of them while Albrecht studied art. They had agreed that they would take it in turns to study. When Albrecht had finished his studies he would work to pay his friend's fees.

Albrecht learnt to paint and to carve wonderful things in wood. The years went by and Albrecht became famous. Now it was his friend's turn, but it was too late. His friend's hands were now so stiff and hard from work that they could never again use a delicate paint-brush.

Albrecht was heart-broken. One day as he watched his friend pray he wished he could make those hands young and soft again. He knew he could not do this, but he could paint them as a tribute, to recognize and say 'Thank you' for his friend's sacrifice.

Activity

Hands are not easy to draw. Try drawing your own hand in pencil. Place your hand on paper and draw round it very lightly. Look closely at the back of your hand and fill in the details.

Exploring Christian Belief

Albrecht's friend held his hands together when praying. Christians do not necessarily hold their hands in that position to pray. Prayer can be said in any position, while working or playing as well as at special prayer times. Albrecht's friend helped him by working. No doubt he also prayed for Albrecht. Christians believe that prayer is a practical way of helping someone. They also believe that sometimes people can be involved in the answer to that prayer. It's no use praying for the hungry if you are not also prepared to help feed them. Prayer and action are two sides of the same coin.

POETRY

ART

Through the Window

Activity

Choose a window in your classroom. Look at its shape very carefully. Draw your window and its frame but **not** the scene through it. How can you get the effect of glass?

Now look through the window. What can you see? Add the scene to the window you drew earlier.

Note   Posters of icons are produced by Fowler Wright publishers. The pack *Christianity: The Orthodox Tradition*, by G. Crow, is very helpful. This may be obtained from South London MultiFaith R.E. Centre, Kilmorie Road, London SE23 2SP.

Icons: A Window on Heaven

Icons are special pictures that some Christians use to help them pray and worship. They are sometimes described as a 'window on heaven'.

When you look at a window your eye does not usually stay on the glass: you look beyond the glass to the scenery you can see through it. In a similar way, if Christians look at an icon it helps them to see beyond the picture. It helps them to understand God himself.

Look at the picture closely. What do you notice about it?

Exploring Christian Belief

Talk over the points the children notice about the icon. An icon is more than a picture: each part has a special meaning and it has to be looked at in a special way.

- The head of the main figure in an icon is usually very round, the nose very straight. This is a symbol of perfection.
- There are no shadows. Shadows represent wrong, sorrow etc. God banishes all wrong.
- There is light around the figure, often called a halo, the light of holiness. 'Holy' means set apart for God, so the figure is someone very special.
- Often, the perspective is reversed in an icon: distant objects get larger rather than smaller. Here the Book of the Gospels appears to reach out because of this. Work will need to be done on perspective in order for children to understand this.

ART

Banners and Kneelers

Banners are extremely popular in churches. You might like to visit a local church that uses banners in worship. Try to find a church that uses embroidered kneelers as well.

In the church, sketch banners and kneelers and colour them in roughly so that you can make a detailed picture later. Alternatively, photograph them.

Underneath your finished drawings write what you think each banner or kneeler is about. You might also like to ask the people who made them what they were trying to say.

Find out when kneelers are used.

Activity

Activity

Design your own banner that expresses something you want to say.

Exploring Christian Belief

Discuss the visit with the children. Ask them how they felt banners and kneelers might help Christians worship. The banners are there to express belief and to help people meditate on a particular idea and aid them in their worship. If the school is a church school, the children might like to design a kneeler for the local church with each child adding a stitch if they want to. Kneeler kits can be bought ready cut but the children can design their own picture. Children might like to investigate designs on altar cloths, vestments and other items used in worship.

Christian Buildings

If possible take the children to visit a number of Christian churches of different types. Try to assess how each building is designed to help people worship; look at, for example, the soaring arches of a cathedral, the plainness of a Quaker meeting-house, the beauty of an Orthodox church.

Worksheets can be designed for local buildings, pointing out particular architectural features. Use cameras and draw sketches to keep a record of these. You can display the pictures when children get back to the classroom. The activity below can be part of the visit.

Activity

Imagine you are a bird above the church. Draw the shape of the church the bird would see.

Exploring Christian Belief

Christians differ over how to use their buildings to help them worship. Many churches are cross-shaped to remind the people of Jesus. Quaker and Brethren meeting-rooms are very plain to avoid distraction, other churches are very ornate to inspire people. Some churches focus on the pulpit and the Bible because that is the centre of their worship, others centre on the altar where Mass/Communion is celebrated.

Assembly Ideas

Make a window frame using card and cling film. Stand different things behind it. Ask the children what they can see through the window. Show an icon poster and explain why icons are called 'windows on heaven'.

Let the children show their hand pictures and tell the story of Albrecht Dürer.

Invite in a group of people who make banners or kneelers for a local church. They might like to bring examples with them and explain the meaning behind them.

Yesuve Saranam

This song is an Indian call to worship. It is sung many times at the start of a service to bring people together to worship God. The words mean 'Jesus, I surrender'. Explain that in this song Christians are singing about 'surrendering' to Jesus as their king or lord.

MUSIC

It's Me, O Lord

This song is a spiritual about prayer.

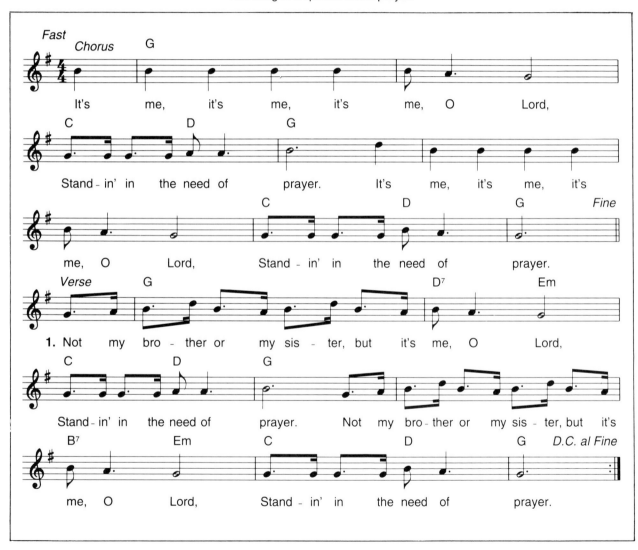

2. Not my mother or my father, but it's me, O Lord . . .

3. Not the stranger or my neighbour, but it's me, O Lord . . .

Exploring Christian Belief

Talk about spending time with people and needing to relax and unwind with them. What sorts of things do families and friends do together? Time spent with people is not time wasted. We should not be working all the time. Prayer and worship are time spent with God. They are vital to any Christian's life. Christians worship God and tell him how great he is, they express their feelings for God in words, in song, drama, ritual and dance. Time spent with God gives them the strength to go out into the world and care for others.

MUSIC

Let Us Break Bread Together

This is a traditional song from the Caribbean about worship.

Arranged by Sue Hatherly

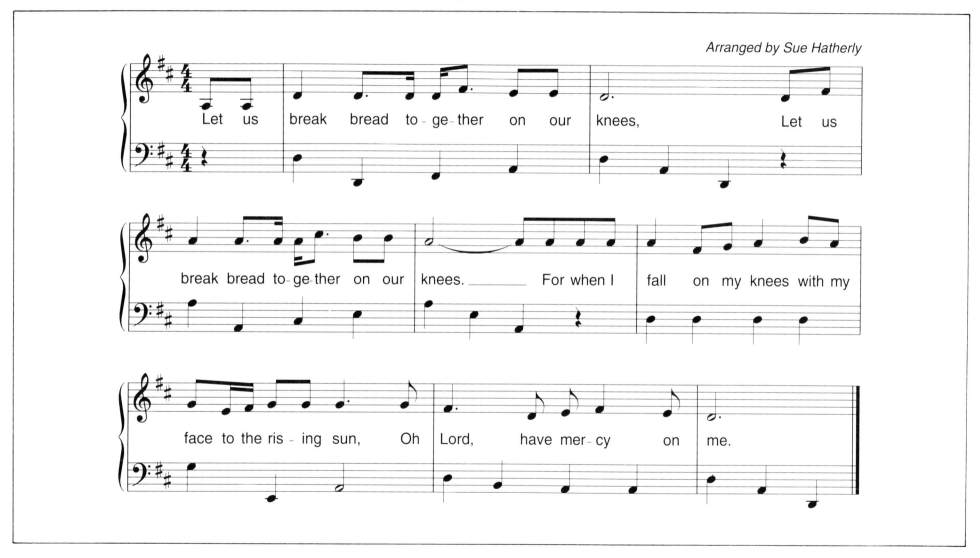

Music for Worship

The Psalms are prayer poems used by Jews and Christians to worship God. Originally they were sung in the Temple in Jerusalem, where various musical instruments would have been used.

This is a modern version of Psalm 150.

Let's praise God with the sound of a
   trumpet,
Tell everyone how good he is with the twang
   of the guitar.
Let's praise God by dancing to the
   tambourine,
Shout his name to the sound of the drums.
Praise God with violins and recorders,
Let cymbals crash the greatness of the Lord
Let every person who breathes praise God.
        (Adapted from Psalm 150)

Activity

Put Psalm 150 to music. After you sing or say each line, play the instruments mentioned in the psalm.

Activity

Draw the instruments mentioned in Psalm 150. Inside each one write what the poet wants to say with that instrument.

Exploring Christian Belief

Discuss the idea of music being a 'language'. Often music can express things we cannot put into words. Christians often use music in worship to help them express their love for God. The following music may be useful for exploring worship:

Elgar's 'The Dream of Gerontius': the chorus 'Praise to the Holiest'.

Handel's 'Messiah': the chorus 'Glory to God'.

Charles Wesley's hymn 'O for a Thousand Tongues': this can be found in most hymn-books.

G. Kendrick's hymn 'God is Good': see *Junior Praise* (Marshall Pickering).

Assembly Ideas

If appropriate, share the songs in assembly. They could alternatively be sung by a group of children.

Talk about how we remember things that are important to us and sing 'Let Us Break Bread Together' (page 113).

Send some messages in assembly by verbal and non-verbal means and use 'It's Me, O Lord' (page 112) to illustrate communication with God.

Make large paper cut-outs of the instruments mentioned in Psalm 150. Children can write in them what the psalmist wants to say with each instrument.

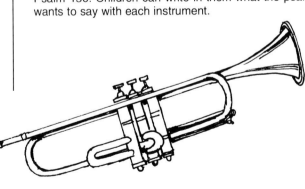

MUSIC

Dance in Worship

King David sometimes danced when he worshipped God. Often when people are happy they 'dance with joy'.

Dance is still used in Christian worship in many ways. Sometimes people just break out into an unplanned dance. At other times dancing is planned, and formal steps are used, or a group of people may dance to some Christian music.

Activity

A Vine Dance

Stand in a space with your feet slightly apart.

Take a step with your right foot in front and to the side of your left foot.

Put your weight on your right foot. Swing your left foot round the back so that it is once again next to your right foot. You should now be standing with your feet slightly apart, as you were when you started.

Now take a step with your right foot behind and to the side of your left foot.

Put your weight on your right foot and swing your left foot round the front so that your feet are back in their original position.

Put both movements together to make a 'vine step'.

Practise the vine step. You will have to move your body as well as your feet or you will look rather stiff! You should also bend your knees as you move your feet.

Join arms with a friend at shoulder height and do the step together. When you are confident, four people can join together and you can add in other steps. For example, you could do several vine steps then a deep knee bend making a circular movement.

Note The 'vine step' may be named thus because it produces a shape that looks like a curling tendril. You might like to link this with 'The Vine' being a title for Jesus: see the topic 'Jesus' (page 74).

DRAMA

Music for the Vine Dance:
When the Spirit of the Lord

Children could sing the words if appropriate. Otherwise just use the melody to accompany the dance.

Arranged by Sue Hatherly

Offering Presents

Worship is about offering and receiving. The worshipper offers God love, adoration, thanks, service, confession and all their troubles and concerns. The worshipper receives love, forgiveness, comfort and strength.

Presents can be offered in many ways:

- Casually • Reluctantly • Fearfully • Joyfully
- With great awe (as if offering the Queen a present)

Presents can also be received in different ways:

- Casually • Disdainfully • Excitedly
- With gratitude • Rejected

Let the children mime or act different ways of offering and receiving presents. They can then choose one situation to develop into a sketch.

Talk about the invisible presents believers offer in worship. Discuss the collection which takes place in many Christian worship services.

Note Some children might like to develop this further, particularly if they are in a church school. Using boxes wrapped as presents, they might like to create a dance in the course of which they place the presents on a table/altar.

Exploring Christian Belief

Worship is offering gifts such as love, adoration, joy and thanks. Christians believe that if these are genuine God will always accept the gift. He will not accept it if the person is harbouring hatred, anger or malice in their heart. Jesus said that if someone came to worship God but bore hatred to their brother they should go back and make it up with their brother, then come and worship God.

Assembly Ideas

Perform the dances with boxes if appropriate. Alternatively perform the sketches.

Encourage some children to perform a vine dance and talk about the use of dance in worship.

DRAMA

Communication

Activity

Communication is getting a message from one person to another.

Look at the drawing below. The two children want to talk to each other but there is a wall between them. The wall stands for all the things that can go wrong in communication.

Draw your own wall. On the bricks of the wall write some of the things which could stop people communicating.

Activity

People need to tell each other how they feel, but often we leave things unsaid. We feel grateful for something someone has done, but fail to tell them. We feel sorry but forget to say so.

Design and make a set of six cards which tell people things we often forget to say. Some can be thank-you cards. Some can be sorry cards. Some can be congratulations cards. Some can be blank for any message you want to put in.

Exploring Christian Belief

Communication is important in any relationship. People are not mind readers: they need to be told that we are sorry, grateful etc. Christians believe that in a relationship with God communication is also important, though he does know what people are feeling. Putting things into words or silent thoughts is part of a friendship with God. There are also few barriers to stop the communication getting through to God. Christians believe God cares; he listens and knows what people want to say even if they cannot put it into words easily.

Note Encourage the children to keep their cards and use them.

PSE

How Some Christians Pray

Hello, my name is Pervin. I live in Pakistan. Although we are Christians we often pray with our heads to the ground as our Muslim neighbours do. When I pray I cover my head with my headscarf to show respect for God.

My name is Ai. I live in Japan. Normally the members of our church spend all of Sunday together sharing meals, enjoying each other's company and praying for each other. In the summer the church members go to camp together so we all know each other very well. Knowing each other so well makes it easier to pray for each other as we know each other's needs.

My name is Philip. I come from South India. The pastor of our church often prays with us. He prayed with my parents when I was born, and he came to pray with the family on my grandfather's birthday. He prayed with us when we moved house and when my elder sister got married. For me, prayer is for all the everyday things of life.

Activity
Interview some Christians in your area and find out what prayer means to them. You might also like to find out how they pray: different Christians pray in different ways.

Cross-curricular Links

Technology

Encourage the children to design a church for a group of Christians. The children should interview some Christians first and ask them how they worship. The children should then design a church that will help them worship in this way. They might need space for drama and dance. They might need room for a small orchestra if the worship uses a lot of music. Show the finished design to the group of Christians and allow them to make any modifications necessary. When the design is finished the children can make a model of the church.

Work on communication using information technology would also be relevant.

Maths

The children can collect data on the number of people who attend local churches, looking also at age and sex. The children would have to look at factors which might influence their survey (major festivals, summer holidays etc). They would also have to decide how long the survey should run to be fair. The results of the survey can be presented in different forms: graphs, pie-charts, diagrams, pictograms etc.

Children could also survey church collections and the uses to which they are put. They could find out the average gift per adult member. This would have to include covenanted donations to be accurate.

Christianity, A World Faith

Christians from different cultures worship in different ways, using forms that suit their situation. If possible invite Christians from a variety of cultures into school and ask them how they worship. Look at the design of churches in other countries and see how they express the same faith through different patterns of architecture.

History

Find out which Christian denominations are represented in the local area, how they came into being and their history.

General Topic Work

This topic would integrate with a topic on communication. *Children First. Book 1* (Wheaton) contains a very detailed topic called 'I've Got a Message to Send'.

Useful Books

My Secret Life, by M. Hebblethwaite (Hunt Thorpe).
Children's Letters to God, by E. Marshall and S. Hample (Collins/Fount).
Learning about Prayer, by Felicity Henderson (Lion).
Learning about the Church, by Felicity Henderson (Lion).
365 Children's Prayers (Lion).
The Story of a Meal, by R. Schindler (St Paul's).
The Church Book, by A. Farnecombe (NCEC).
When Christians Meet (CEM). An exploration of multi-cultural Christianity.
Christian Buildings and *Churches in Britain* (CEM).
Exploring a Church (CEM). A set of 24 work-cards. An excellent resource for helping children both to explore a church building and to understand the worship which happens there.
Teaching Christianity, by H. Thacker (Palm Tree). A photo-copyable book containing lots of useful information and accompanying pictures which teachers can use to form their own worksheets. There is a section on worship, prayer and the church.
Sent by the Lord and *Many and Great* (Wild Goose Publications). Multicultural Christian songs. Available in tape or book form from Chansitor Publications Ltd, St Mary's Works, St Mary's Plain, Norwich NR3 3BH.

The Hand Game

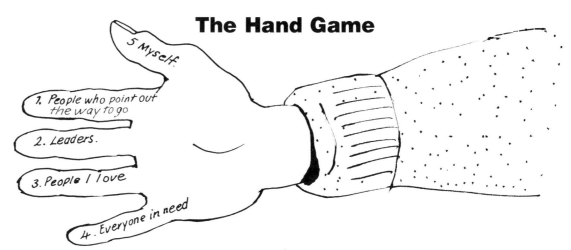

Christian children sometimes use a hand to help them to pray. Each finger on the hand reminds them to pray for different people.

1. The index or pointing finger reminds them to pray for people who help them: people who 'point out' the way to go in life. Who do you think the children pray for when looking at this finger?

2. The middle finger reminds them to pray for leaders. Why do you think this finger represents leaders?

3. The ring finger is the finger on which married people wear a wedding-ring. This finger reminds the children to pray for people they love such as parents and friends.

4. The little finger reminds them to pray for all in need.

5. Last, they look at the thumb. This is when Christian children pray for themselves. Why do you think this is left to last?

Activity

Draw round your hand. **Either** write in each finger what a Christian child would pray for, **or** make up your own finger game where each finger stands for a different prayer.

When you have finished make a display of everyone's hands.

Exploring Christian Belief

Christians believe it is important to pray for others. They believe God answers prayer but they also believe that they have their part to play. It would be wrong to pray for the hungry and not do anything about feeding them.

CROSS-CURRICULAR LINKS   **GAMES**

Pretzels

In many countries snacks called **pretzels** are very popular. A legend says the shape represents praying hands.

Activity

You can make soft pretzels using a basic bread recipe.

Shape the dough into 'sausages' and tie each one into a loose knot as shown. You can make the bread stick where it crosses over by brushing with a little milk.

When the pretzels are well risen, brush the tops with a little water and sprinkle with (low sodium) salt and sesame seeds. Bake for about 15 minutes.

Pretzels are sometimes given as a present. If you want to do this, you can tie them with a ribbon as people do on the Continent.

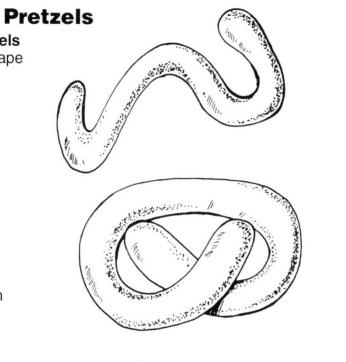

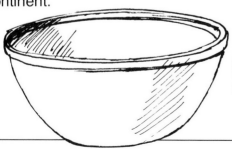

Think About It

The shape of a pretzel is said to be like praying hands. If you pray, do you find it helpful to pray in a certain way?

Exploring Christian Belief

Christians believe that people can pray at any time and in any way. God is prepared to listen and knows what people want to say even before they have said it. That does not mean people do not need to pray: prayer, like conversation, is part of a Christian's relationship with God.

Note There is a basic bread recipe in *Christianity Topic Book 1*, pages 62–63. Halve this recipe for a smaller group.

Activity

At Easter in parts of Germany, the pretzel shape is pulled into a heart and ribbons are attached.

You might like to make some of these special pretzels at Easter. Why do you think a heart shape is used?

Note See pages 35, 66 and 67 for more Easter recipes.

COOKING